To my girls.
Without them, I wouldn't be much.

—Mike Bianchi

To Jessica.
You make my life more colorful
and my light shine brighter.

—Danny Wuerffel

CONTENTS

FOREWORD

I first saw Danny Wuerffel in person as he was warming up before the Florida State High School Championship game between his Ft. Walton Beach Vikings and St. Thomas Aquinas at "the Swamp" in 1991.

As he was throwing the ball in warmups before the game, Danny would drop the ball way behind his head with his right elbow pointing toward the sky. I remember telling Gator assistant coach John Reaves, who was sitting with me: "I don't believe this young man is a good enough passer to play big-time college football."

Then the game started and Danny did not drop the ball behind his head. His passes were quick and sharp and seemed to hit his receivers in perfect stride, right between the number on their jerseys, just about every time. I was amazed as Danny led his team to a 39-14 victory over a much more talented St. Thomas team. He had three touchdown passes and also an 80-yard run for a score.

After the game, I met Danny personally and began the most inspired recruiting effort that I probably ever accomplished. As we all know, Danny Wuerffel became the best passer in the history of college football, but most importantly he helped direct the Florida Gators to four Southeastern Conference championships in his four years, and the 1996 national championship in New Orleans. He was phenomenal in our 52-20 victory over FSU.

The best quality about Danny is that he is one of the most sincere Christians I've ever met. He shares his faith and conviction to all, but he does not force it on anyone. I have not heard anybody who has had anything negative to say about Danny as a person.

The one play that I remember that exemplified Danny's ability was in the national championship game against FSU. The score was 24-20, our favor, and we had the ball third and seven in the third quarter at the FSU 7-yard line. A touchdown would obviously be huge at this point, as a field goal would have only put us up by seven.

We called timeout and I was trying to figure out a play to throw into the end zone for a score. We decided to put Reidel Anthony and Ike Hilliard on the same side in our four-wide receiver package. Reidel was to clear straight through and Ike would run a slant behind him and hopefully catch the ball and dive into the end zone.

As the play unfolded, I noticed their middle linebacker was dropping right into the slant area where Ike would be. Also, our left guard got beat on the play and the FSU defensive tackle was charging untouched straight at Danny.

Danny threw the ball into the area and this is what happened: The FSU defensive tackle hit Danny as he released the ball. The FSU middle linebacker stretched to knock the ball down and missed by inches. The FSU defensive back was on Ike's back. The ball hit Ike right in the chest on the 3- or 4-yard line, and he somehow squirmed away from the defensive back to dive into the end zone to give us a 31-20 lead that proved to be insurmountable.

I've said many times that I believe that every ball Danny threw, he had 10,000 angels directing and protecting his pass.

I believe God chose Danny to be the most productive and efficient passer in the history of college football. Danny, in return, has always given the Lord credit for his success, as well as his teammates and coaches.

Danny is continuing to do God's work as his ministry for Jesus Christ spreads throughout our country.

In the Florida Gator Nation, Danny is the most heralded player ever, the biggest star football player in the history of our University. His accomplishments—all his records and his championships—will likely never be matched.

Danny Wuerffel is "The Florida Gator Football Star."

—*Steve Spurrier*

1

RECRUITING: BECOMING A GATOR

IN THE BEGINNING

often tell people I became a Gator because of the experience I had with the red phone. You see, when I was recruited out of Fort Walton Beach High School, I narrowed my choices down to three schools—Alabama, Florida State and Florida.

I made my first official visit to Alabama. Gene Stallings coached the Crimson Tide at the time, and after a couple of days touring the campus and athletic facilities, he brought me into his office, showed me a red phone and asked if I knew why it was so significant. I hadn't a clue. "Well," Coach Stallings said, "the red phone is to talk to God, and at Alabama we get a discounted rate of $1,000 per minute." Naturally, I was very impressed.

The next week, I visited Florida State and sure enough Bobby Bowden had a red phone in his office, too, and he told me that the Seminoles get a discounted rate to talk to God—a rate of a $1,000 per minute. Again, I was very impressed.

Then the next week, I visited Florida and Coach Spurrier called me into his office and showed me his red phone and asked, "Danny, do you know what this phone is for?" I nodded my head. "I sure do, Coach. That's the phone where you can talk to God."

"That's right," Coach Spurrier said. "You're a smart kid. Do you know how much it costs to talk to God?"

"I sure do," I replied. "It costs $1,000 per minute."

Coach Spurrier shook his head.

"No," he said. "It's free here in Gainesville, because it's a local call."

And that's why I chose Florida. At least that's my story, and I'm sticking to it.

THE SWAMP MEET

Actually, my first *trip* to Florida Field came when I was a junior in high school. My high school football coach was Jimmy Ray Stephens, a former University of Florida player who would also coach the offensive line at UF during my years in Gainesville.

He came to Ft. Walton High at the end of my sophomore year, when we finished 3-7. He came from Williston High School, where he turned that program around in one year. In one half of the spring jamboree at Williston, the Red Devils scored more points than they had in the entire previous season. Coach Stephens brought that same sort of offensive innovation and explosiveness to the Fort Walton Beach Vikings. His first year—my junior year—we went 8-2, and our second year we went 14-0 and won the state title.

Coach Stephens and I celebrating after we won the district champion-ship in Fort Walton Beach.

My first unofficial trip to Florida came with Coach Stephens during my junior year. It was homecoming and I went to my first Gator Growl the night before the game. I remember pulling into Gainesville with Coach Stephens, his wife Regina and one of our other players and we were singing along to Van Morrison's "Brown Eyed Girl" on the car stereo. I don't know how good the rendition of the song was, but it was a great trip.

FIRST GAME AT THE SWAMP

My first game at Ben Hill Griffin Stadium was not as a Gator. It was actually during my senior season of high school when we played the state championship game at Florida Field.

We went into the game 13-0, and we played Ft. Lauderdale St. Thomas Aquinas. We walked out onto the field, and it felt a little bit like we were Jack climbing the beanstalk and ending up in the land of the giants. St. Thomas Aquinas was a private school that had 11 or 12 guys sign Division 1-A scholarships after that season. Private schools, as you know, are always accused of recruiting the best players in their area. So when we walked out to midfield for the coin toss, in order to look our opponents in the eyes, we all had to look up—like David when he was about to face Goliath.

Our first touchdown, believe it or not, came on a triple option play when one of their defenders missed an assignment and I ran 79 yards for a touchdown. Nobody thought I had the speed to run like that, but I was actually a pretty fair runner in my day.

We were a run-and-shoot type of team, but we also ran quite a bit of option and mixed in a lot of motion in the backfield. I had two runs during my senior season of more than 75 yards and I ran for two scores in the state title game. We ended up winning the game 39-14, and I can still remember Coach Stephens and me crying like little kids after we won the state championship. My perform-ance that day caught the eye of an up-and-coming head coach at Florida by the name of Spurrier, who was in the stands watching my performance.

You know, Coach Spurrier not only quarterbacked the Gators in college, I'm told he won the Heisman Trophy by making a last-second 40-yard field goal against Auburn in 1966. Who knows, maybe it was my kicking more than my passing that caught his attention during the state title game. I was the back-up kicker in high school and during the pregame warmups, I booted an extra point so far into the north end zone stands that it hit the long, narrow scoreboard above the lower level and knocked out several lights. OK, so it wasn't quite as dramatic as Roy Hobbs and the exploding scoreboard in the movie *The Natural*, but for the next two or three years at UF, I could still see the busted lights that I broke during the state championship game. I haven't told anybody about those busted lights until now. (I hope athletic director Jeremy Foley doesn't bill me now that he knows).

FLORIDA, FLORIDA STATE, OR ALABAMA

I guess I can admit this now, but I actually used to be a Florida State fan. I even have a picture of myself when I was in high school wearing an FSU cap. This, of course, was before I saw the light. All of us have been confused at one point or another in our lives.

Even after we won the state championship in Gainesville, I didn't know for sure that I was going to end up at the University of Florida. I had three official recruiting visits that I took before I made my decision. My first trip was to Alabama, and I went in the middle of the week because I had a couple days off from school. As it turned out, I was the only recruit there, and I remember they walked me into the locker room and had a jersey with my name on it. This greatly impressed me and I remember thinking, "Wow, they really must want me at Alabama." I didn't know at the time that every school put your name on a jersey. Still, my trip to Alabama was a great experience. I liked Coach Stallings. He was a well respected man, and I had a lot of admiration for him. Former Alabama quarterback Jay Barker was my host, and I appreciated him and what he stood for as a Christian athlete.

They gave me the Bear Bryant treatment at Alabama, and one of their biggest selling points was the Bear's legacy and all the history and tradition at the school. Their recruiting pitch—

at least in my mind—was, "Don't you want to come to Alabama, where you could possibly be the first person to lead us to our 11th national championship?" While Alabama's tradition was impressive, I started asking myself a different question, "Wouldn't I like to be the quarterback to lead Florida State or especially Florida to their FIRST national championship?" That seemed more appealing.

The next week, I went to Florida State, where my sister Sara was enrolled. She had started at FSU in 1989, which meant she was in Tallahassee all during my high school career. That was an advantage for FSU. I spent a lot of time visiting my sister, and Ft. Walton Beach is much closer to Tallahassee than Gainesville. Like I said, earlier in my life, before I knew any better, I gravitated toward being a Florida State fan. In fact, one of the lowest moments of my freshman year of high school came when one of my friends—a die-hard Gator fan—asked me to sign his yearbook and I ended up drawing a picture of a Seminole stabbing a Gator. My friend has since shown me that picture many times over the years just to rag on me. What a sad memory! A true skeleton in my Gator closet.

I had a great visit to Florida State and really enjoyed my time there. After my first trip to Tallahassee, I was definitely leaning toward Florida State. However, I think a sign from heaven foreshadowed that FSU might not be the right place for me. My parents brought our dog with us on the visit, and as we were leaving, the dog squatted and peed right on the shoe of FSU recruiting coordinator Ronnie Cottrell. You could say our dog quite literally rained on FSU's parade.

My last trip was to Florida, where I went and had another great experience. Shane Matthews and his girlfriend Stephanie—now his wife—were my hosts. Little did I know then that I would end up spending several seasons with Shane as a teammate. We played one season together at UF, and then we hooked up again in the NFL with the Chicago Bears and the

My dog, Chester, and I kayaking in Joe's Bayou behind my parents' house in Destin, Florida.

Washington Redskins. They still tease me that I was the only recruit who asked to go to the movies instead of heading out to the night clubs. My wife Jessica and I have become good friends with the Matthews, and Shane and I team up with former Gator great Kerwin Bell to run a quarterback camp and passing academy in Ocala each summer for high school athletes.

As you can probably guess, it was a great visit to UF and I left there fairly confused. I really enjoyed myself and liked Alabama, Florida State and Florida.

I was trying to be very careful in my decision, which is why I didn't want to commit to any of the schools right after a visit. I knew it was best to get back home and think about it. Plus, I wanted to meet with each of the head coaches one more time at my home.

The thing that stood out about Coach Stallings's home visit was that he kept saying, "If we just had the right quarterback, we'd throw the ball a lot more at Alabama." At the time,

Alabama was a running-oriented, defensive-minded team that rarely threw the ball down the field, and that was a major concern for me. Finally, my dad pressed Coach Stallings on the issue by asking him: "If it was the perfect world and you had the ideal quarterback and you could throw the ball as much as you wanted, how many yards per game would your quarterback throw for?" Coach Stallings thought a minute and said, "With the right quarterback and the ideal situation, we'd throw for 200 yards a game." My dad and I looked at each other and shared the same thought—200 yards a game was about a quarter and a half at Florida.

SPURRIER AND BOWDEN

Bobby Bowden is certainly a great recruiter, and I think recruiters would make fine politicians. They have this knack of meeting new people, making small talk and appearing as if they know you really well. Coach Bowden is great at small talk, but sometimes even the best of them put their foot in their mouth.

Coach Bowden walked into our house and I introduced him to my dad as an Air Force Chaplain. "So," Coach Bowden said to my dad, "you're a man of the cloth." My dad nodded and answered. "Yes, I am." Then, after meeting my entire family, Coach Bowden said to my father, "So, are you Catholic?" This is obviously an awkward question to answer, for Catholic priests can't get married or have children. My dad sort of smiled and said he thought about becoming a Catholic priest, but the whole celibacy thing sort of ruled that out for him. As soon as Bobby Bowden asked my dad if he was Catholic, you could see (FSU defensive coordinator and the assistant coach in charge of recruiting me) Mickey Andrews sort of bite his lip in embarrassment. As it turned out, Coach Andrews came after me hard in high school and came after me even harder when I became the quarterback at Florida.

Anyway, Coach Spurrier was the last coach to visit my home and he came up with assistant coach Bob Sanders. They planned to fly into a little airport in Destin on UF's small private plane. It was a very foggy night and it turned out to be too dangerous to land in Destin, so they landed in Niceville, a little town about 45 minutes away. Coach Spurrier went to a lot of trouble to come to my house, and that was very impressive.

I would say the difference between Coach Spurrier and Coach Bowden's recruiting approach is that Bobby Bowden tends to be more of a typical Southern good ol' boy. He's homey and folksy and seems to enjoy himself in crowds. Coach Spurrier was more direct and said things from the heart. Like, for instance, when I was being recruited, the Gators lost to Notre Dame in the Sugar Bowl. Coach was really frustrated with the offense and told me he thought I could have come in and thrown seven TDs that night. Coach Spurrier sold his football program and his offense more than anything else.

The opportunity to play for Steve Spurrier was one of the key reasons I chose the Gators. He'd already had incredible success with quarterbacks at Duke, UF and even as a professional coach in the United States Football League. I wanted to play in his type of offense, even though the competition at Florida seemed like it would be more intense to win the starting job. The Gators already had a highly touted young quarterback on the roster named Terry Dean. All Florida State had was a little-known basketball player who also happened to play quarterback—some guy named Charlie Ward.

Florida was also the best fit for me as an academic institution. There were more opportunities and majors at UF for me to choose from, which turned out to be very important. In high school, I was totally undecided on what degree I wanted to pursue and I ended up switching majors several times.

During the recruiting process, I kept asking myself, "If you weren't playing football, which school would you choose?" The answer was the University of Florida.

Even though it was a very tough and confusing decision, my mom gave me a piece of advice back then that I still use today. She said, "Danny, you can always make a decision and second guess yourself for a long time. Think about your decision, pray about it and make the best decision you can at the time. And then after you make your decision, you go about your business as if there were never any other choices to begin with."

Why is it that moms always say the best things?

2

TRAINING CAMP '92: I WANNA GO HOME

When I was in high school, we had some seriously tough practices. Coach Stephens took us off into the wilderness for a mini training camp-like experience. We took an old pasture, removed most of the thicket, and had a makeshift football field. We were roughing it, for sure, and it was tough, but not even that could have prepared me for the gruelling, gut-wrenching experience of my first two-a-day practices at the University of Florida.

Most of the other freshman football players arrived in Gainesville during the second summer term, but I decided to stay home in Destin the entire summer before going off to college. It was a wonderful summer spent on the water almost every day—water skiing, swimming—just having a great time. The summer of 1992 was one of the highlights of my childhood. The freedom to relax and wind down was terrific. No summer athletic leagues, early morning workouts or anything. I also worked hard to stay in shape, but little did I know what awaited me at UF's training camp.

SHAVED HEADS AND SORE FEET

The upperclassmen showed us a warm welcome, demanding that we shave our heads bald or face serious consequences. We weren't exactly sure what that meant, and we really didn't want to find out. So we got some hair clippers, gathered together in one of the rooms in Yon Hall, leaned over a trash can and went to town. I've heard people like Mike Bianchi say bald is beautiful, but let me tell you I've never seen so many ugly heads in all my life. Trouble is, now I'm 30 years old and my head is starting to look more and more like it did back then, but with no clippers needed. It's a gradual, all-natural cleansing of the scalp. Hopefully, bald IS beautiful. I'll find out really soon.

The day before two-a-days started, I had to take a strength test, which included the dreaded squat max. The assistant strength coach put 350 pounds on the bar—he had the easy job. My job was to do as many full squats as I could with what seemed like a small vehicle on my back. I ended up doing it 10 times, which I thought was pretty impressive. The problem was I woke up the next morning with the sorest and most aching muscles of my life. To make matters worse, that was the same morning we had the infamous 12-minute run—Coach Spurrier's own conditioning test. This was Coach's baby. He always felt a 12-minute run provided a great way to evaluate the overall conditioning of an athlete. Other coaches would argue that other conditioning tests are better suited for football players, but Coach Spurrier, a runner himself, was committed to the 12-minute run.

Coach Spurrier loved being in shape and was a big believer in nutrition. He was a healthy eater, and he wanted us to be healthy eaters, too. Living in the dorm and eating with the

Here I am dropping back to throw in pregame warm-ups.

coaches in the dining hall, I learned very quickly that if Coach Spurrier came around, you needed to be very careful about what you had on your plate. He would actually walk around and critique what the players were eating. I was like everyone else during my freshman year. I'd go through the line, grab a couple of hamburgers, a few chicken wings and, if I really wanted to be healthy, I'd load up on the french fries. But by my senior year when Coach Spurrier came around, I learned to always have a lot of color on my plate—a lot of yellows and greens, fruits and vegetables. In 1996, I was having lunch with Billy Young, one of the young quarterbacks, when Coach Spurrier came up and looked disapprovingly at Billy's plate. "Billy," Coach Spurrier said in that twang of his, "you don't have any vegetables on that plate. You need to have some color on your plate like Danny here. Right, Danny?"

Anyway, back to the 12-minute run. The idea is that each position player has a minimum distance he must cover in 12 minutes—except the distance isn't so minimal. I think the quarterbacks had to cover something close to TWO MILES. All I know is that it was an absolutely miserable experience. My legs hurt so badly because of the squat test; I had sharp pains shooting up and down my legs with each step. Somehow, though, I managed to gut it out and make my time. There was no way I was going to fail my first day in front of Coach Spurrier and my teammates.

Before the first practice, the athletic trainers made it very clear that it was mandatory for every player to have their ankles taped for each practice. I wasn't accustomed to having tape tightly wrapped around my ankles, and this just made matters worse. The tape caused blisters, and let me tell you, blisters on your feet are no fun. So let's review the situation: My legs felt like Jell-O, my muscles were on fire and my feet hurt. And practice hadn't even started yet. What had I gotten myself into?

The pain continued through the start of two-a-days. At the beginning of each practice, instead of having just football drills, we had the "County Fair", which was about 12 different agility stations where the coaches had us running through ropes and around tires, hitting the ground and popping up, and certainly making our lives miserable. After the first couple of days of this stuff, I could barely walk. I remember constantly walking around singing the Beach Boys song, "I Wanna Go Home." You know, even though I spent my high school years on Florida's Gulf Coast, I never considered myself a Beach Boy. But the song seemed awfully appropriate at that time.

MOVING INTO YON HALL

When I first arrived at UF, the NCAA still allowed athletic dorms, and the football players lived in Yon Hall, a dorm built into the east side of the stadium; very convenient for the athletes.

My roommate was Jason Odom, an offensive lineman whom I met on my recruiting trip to Florida. He was soft-spoken, kind and very large—six-foot-five, 285 pounds to be exact. Even today, he remains one of my greatest friends. We hit it off so well on our recruiting trip that we decided to room together if we both went to Florida. In fact, when Coach Spurrier found out Jason had already verbally committed to UF, he commissioned Jason to call and put the sales pitch on me. I tease Jason and say he was a better recruiter than Spurrier and Bowden combined.

Jason arrived at Yon Hall during the Summer B term, which meant he got first dibs on the room since I didn't arrive until training camp. It was a very small room, but that didn't matter to Jason: He arrived at UF with a king-size waterbed and put it all the way up to the middle half of the room, which meant just his bed took up his whole side. So, of course, his other belongings spilled over into my half of the room. As it turned out, I ended up getting about a half of a half of a room. This didn't seem quite fair to me, but I didn't say a word because I remembered something my dad once told me: "Always honor and respect your linemen." So I didn't complain, and that may have been one of the best decisions I ever made. Jason Odom ended up protecting my left side all through college, and he did a tremendous job of it.

We had some memorable experiences in the dorm—some good, some bad. Many nights, Jason would enjoy staying up late, watching TV, drinking Mountain Dew and eating Oreos. After living with him for a couple of years, I think I saw every episode of The Brady Bunch and watched the movie Goonies about 200 times. I can remember being so tired and fatigued, but unable to sleep because Jason had the TV blaring and he would loudly tear open the Oreo bags and gulp down the Mountain Dew. Then, all of the sudden, he would just crash like a big grizzly bear going into hibernation. Meanwhile, I'd be so wired that I'd be up for hours frustrated with him.

But even though I rarely complained and tried to be kind, frustration usually finds a way to surface. One of the most coveted items from the dining hall was chocolate milk (cartons of chocolate milk were prized possessions and hard to come by). One morning, after a miserable night of sleep courtesy of my Mountain Dew-gulping, Oreo-chomping grizzly bear of a roommate, I opened the refrigerator in our dorm room:

> "And what to my wandering eyes did appear...
> a chocolate milk carton, with no grizzly bear near."

In a moment of dire thirst, roommate frustration, and sleep deprivation, I stole Jason's chocolate milk and savored every chug of it.

PING-PONG CHAMPION AND GATORADE GRINCH

Jason and I ended up having a relationship like two brothers. We had some great times together and would spend many late hours playing ping-pong in Yon Hall. We had many knock-down, drag-out ping-pong tournaments. Jason and I, along with our kicker Bart Edmiston, would stay up for hours and hours around that ping-pong table. Bart said the freshman semester ping-pong hours got him so far behind in school he had to work his butt off his last few years to make up enough ground to get into medical school. For me, though, all those hours of ping-pong paid off years later: I ended up winning the Washington Redskins Ping-Pong Tournament during the 2003 preseason. Unfortunately, this was one of the highlights of my NFL career.

Even though it was convenient, Yon Hall was not the most luxurious place. One summer, the air conditioning went out and it was blistering hot. Everybody in Yon was miserable, but Jason and I were industrious sorts. We came up with an idea to make our own air conditioning. We went and got several milk crates, stacked them up and lined the bottom one with a garbage bag. We filled the crates with ice from the machine by our room, pointed the fan at our contraption, turned it on and—voila!— we had cool air blowing on us. The only thing we should have added was a siphon hose so we could drain the melted ice from the bottom of the garbage bag out the window.

Athletes, as you can imagine, get hungry and thirsty at all hours of the day and night. Well, game days were one of the few times that they'd give you unlimited Gatorade because they obviously wanted you to stay hydrated. There were some people like punter Shayne Edge who took advantage of the unlimited Gatorade on game days, and he packed his bag full of the stuff and brought it back to Yon Hall. I'm telling you, he had a refrigerator filled with hundreds of Gatorades, and yet he was the stingiest guy on the planet. He was the Gatorade Grinch. I mean, he would never, ever share his Gatorade with you. You had a better chance of getting Coach Spurrier to run the ball on third down than getting a Gatorade from Shayne Edge. Later in my career at UF, Shayne finally gave me a Gatorade, and it was such an honor I wouldn't even drink it. Instead, I put it in my car and left it there for about two years as a memento. I ended up presenting it to Jason several years later, and we got a great laugh.

MOVING INTO THE REAL WORLD

I can't tell you how many great memories I have and wonderful friendships I developed during those years in the dorm. I remember Bart Edmiston putting his bed up on blocks so he would have room to put his stuff underneath. Jeff Mitchell and Donnie Young actually built a wall in their room separating the beds from the TV. Or Errict Rhett and those snakes he used to have in his room. I don't know what kind of snakes they were—maybe boa constrictors—but I do know they were big and scary.

During my years at UF, Yon Hall was phased out because the NCAA no longer allowed athletic dorms. As young players away from home for the first time, we had some great bonding experiences in those old, cramped rooms at Yon Hall, but we were all happy to be leaving. While it was convenient to live at the stadium, Yon was old, small and rundown. We moved into an on-campus apartment after we left Yon Hall. It was a modest place with four small rooms, two bathrooms, a living room and a kitchen. But you wouldn't have known it was modest. We thought we had moved into a palace.

One of my neatest memories from our new abode was movie night on Flavet Field—a large field right behind our apartment. They brought out huge speakers and set up a gigantic movie screen, and on this particular night they were showing a double feature—*The Lion King* and *Forrest Gump*. People came from all over that night with blankets and lawn chairs to watch the movies. Jason Odom, of course, was my roommate and he wasn't going to bother with any blankets or lawn chairs. He just picked up the sofa from our apartment, put it over his shoulder, hauled it out to the field and we watched the movie in style. Yes, there are certain advantages to living with a 300-pound mountain of a man.

There was, however, one drawback to moving out of the athletic dorms: No privacy. We had great success on the field during my junior and senior seasons, and sometimes it's hard going to school every day with 40,000 of your greatest fans and then living on campus in an accessible place where people know your address. The most overwhelming times came at the end of the fall semester my senior season, right after I won the Heisman Trophy. What would be a better Christmas present for everyone in your Gator family than something autographed by Danny, right? We used to have rows of people knocking on our door, sheepishly asking for an autograph and then pulling out 15 items to sign. It was really sort of an overwhelming experience for me, and sometimes it seemed like more than I could handle.

But I'd rather have it that way than the other. I was very blessed that so many fans supported me and continue to support me. This might sound corny or contrived, but it really is great to be a Florida Gator.

3

DOERING'S GOT A TOUCHDOWN: MY FRESHMAN SEASON

MIRACLE IN THE BLUEGRASS

One of the highlights of my 18-year football career—from the seventh grade all the way through the NFL—came my freshman year at the University of Kentucky. We were heavily favored to beat the Kentucky Wildcats, and for whatever reason, things weren't going well at all. Terry Dean started the game and had thrown a couple of interceptions, so Coach Spurrier inserted me into the game in the second quarter just to see if he could change things up a bit. Unfortunately, it didn't change things much at all. On my first play, I overthrew a middle route for an interception.

So Terry went right back in, playing into the third quarter and, in the process, threw a couple more interceptions. When he threw his fourth interception in the fourth quarter, out went Terry again and in came Danny. This time, we quickly drove down the field. I threw a TD pass to Chris Doering, and we were on our way for a great comeback. But I wasn't done making mistakes.

We had a little pass play called that was supposed to go to the left side, and I remember Coach Spurrier saying, "Now, Danny, just be careful with this one." I was real careful all right—careful to throw it right to the defender for my second interception of the game. On the next series, I dropped back to pass, looked to my right, and saw what looked to be a wide-open Chris Doering streaking across the middle of the field (Note to readers: "Streaking" is a term that has a couple of connotations. One of them refers to running really fast, but if you know Chris, another definition would work just as well. He's a little crazy like that.) I couldn't get the ball to him fast enough. Well, right in front of me, there were three big linemen who were blocking my vision of the middle linebacker who happened to be standing right in line with Chris the Streaker. I threw a perfect pass right to the linebacker.

A lot of times when I watch games on TV, the announcers will say, "What in the world was the quarterback looking at? He threw it right to the defender." Well, I knew exactly what I was looking at—the backs of some very large men. Things look a lot different from the stands and on TV than they do when you're on the field in the land of giants, trying to look past them to complete a pass. And often you just have to guess what's happening on the other side, let it fly, and hope for the best. But enough of the excuses: The bottom line was, I had just thrown my third interception of the game.

DOERING'S GOT A TOUCHDOWN!

I think Coach Spurrier was just flabbergasted at this point. Terry had thrown four interceptions and I had thrown three.

That's right; we had SEVEN interceptions with about a minute left to play. And to this day, I'm not really sure why Coach put me back into the game, but I am very thankful he did.

After Kentucky kicked a field goal, Harrison Houston made a great kickoff return all the way out to our 42-yard line. I threw a couple of passes to Jack Jackson and Errict Rhett, getting us down to the Kentucky 28-yard line with 26 seconds left. We called a timeout, and Coach Spurrier put in four wide receivers, called four "go" routes and told me to throw the ball to Jack Jackson on the sideline. I went back to pass, tried to look off the safety, turned and fired it out to Jack. It didn't work. The safety closed on the ball and knocked it down.

So now there are only eight seconds left—time for one more play to avoid the biggest upset of the Coach Spurrier era. Nobody expected to be in this situation. In fact, Jim Watson, one of our offensive linemen said after the game, "If you had told me three weeks ago, we were going to have to make a miracle play, I would have said it was very unlikely. But, then, three weeks ago I would have told you that I was expecting to spend the second half on the bench, watching the second team finishing the game for us."

It was third and 10 from the Kentucky 28. Jack Jackson and Chris Doering were split to the right; Aubrey Hill and Harrison Houston to the left. Coach Spurrier called the same play as before. He wanted the wide receivers to run four "go" routes and I was supposed to throw it to Jack again. And that was my intention as I dropped back to pass—look off the safety, turn and throw it to Jack. I don't know why, but at the last millisecond I just had this feeling that the safety was going to jump all over Jack. So I gave a quick pump fake in Jack's direction and turned and threw the ball down the middle of the field, where Chris Doering somehow was wide open. You want to talk about a great moment? From the highlights that came on later, I can still hear Mick Hubert, the radio voice of the Gators, yelling out:

Much of our offense was based on calling audibles like this one against the Georgia Bulldogs. *(Photo courtesy of Florida Sports Information)*

"DOERING'S GOT A TOUCHDOWN! DOERING'S GOT A TOUCHDOWN! OH MY! DOERING'S GOT A TOUCHDOWN! THE GATORS HAVE TAKEN THE LEAD! UNBELIEVABLE! CHRIS DOERING'S GOT A TOUCHDOWN!"

Chris had a great knack for being in the right place at the right time, and what a great moment that was for both of us. We'd both overcome some adversity. I was a 19-year-old quarterback who'd just thrown three interceptions and was one week removed from my first college game. Chris was an unwanted prep receiver who spent two years as a walk-on trying to earn a scholarship at the University of Florida.

The team swarmed the field and it was just an amazing atmosphere. To this day, I still can't believe the Wildcats were in the coverage they were in—a soft Cover 2. "When the ball was thrown," Chris said afterward, "I couldn't believe there was nobody near me."

The Wildcats could have had four or five defenders in the end zone, but they stuck with only two deep defenders, and am I ever glad they did!

AN ANXIOUS GATOR

The week after the Kentucky game, Coach Spurrier had a huge decision to make: Who was he going to start against Tennessee—Terry or me? After careful deliberation, analysis and scrutinizing of game tapes (OK, he probably flipped a coin), Coach made the decision to go with me. And what an incredibly stressful week it turned out to be. I still remember experiencing great anxiety, so much so that I actually found myself feeling physically ill at different times during the week. It was one of the few times, actually the only time, where I felt emotionally overwhelmed prior to a game.

When we ran out onto Florida Field, it was one of those amazing crystal clear, sunny and blue Saturday afternoons at the Swamp. We played against the mighty Volunteers, ranked No. 5 in the country, and their star quarterback, Heath Shuler, who threw for 355 yards and five touchdowns that day. I remember him making some incredibly stellar plays, like running all the way to his right, turning and launching a missile all the way back across the field for a long touchdown.

But we jumped ahead 21-0, and Tennessee had to play from behind all game. Coach Spurrier designed a game plan that was very comfortable for me in my first start. I had a good game, threw for three touchdowns and, more importantly, I took care of the ball. I only threw one interception and didn't make many mistakes, which was a priority after the seven interceptions we threw against Kentucky.

After the game, a reporter asked my high school coach Jimmy Ray Stephens (who that year became the offensive line coach at UF) what made me tick, and he said I have an "inner conceit." My father was asked the same question and he said, "Spiritual calm." I don't know exactly what made me overcome the intense anxiety of my first start. I just remember lying in my room after the game absolutely drained, physically and emotionally, but just so thankful and proud to have been a part of that great day.

BROKEN RECORDS AND ACHING BACKS

With my first start behind me, I started to really get comfortable the following week in a 38-24 victory against Mississippi State. I had one of those amazing days where everything just seemed to work perfectly. By the time it was over, I had thrown for 449 yards and broken the great Kerwin Bell's school record for passing yards in a game.

LSU was next. I was gaining more confidence each day, and I was looking forward to our trip to the bayou. But early in the week, I started feeling sharp pains in my back. I went to our

Here I am warming up for the next drive on the sidelines.
(Photo courtesy of Florida Sports Information)

trainers and they put me on a regimen of massages and therapy, but the pain still remained when we flew to Baton Rouge. In our walk-through the day before the game, I was really hurting and asked Rich Tuten, our strength and conditioning coach, to help stretch out my back. As he stretched my knees toward my shoulders, my back actually started feeling worse and got even tighter. Then I did something a quarterback should never do: I went and played catch with a lineman. Jason Odom and I were tossing the ball back and forth when he threw a wounded duck high and over my shoulder. When I jumped up to try to catch it, my whole lower back began to spasm. I could barely walk and couldn't bend over. I couldn't even bend over far enough to take a snap, which can be a bit of a problem if you're a quarterback.

We went back to the hotel and the trainers gave me some medicine. I didn't go with the team to the movie or the pregame meeting. I lay in bed and even had to get the trainer to bring me dinner. The next morning, I didn't think I was going to be able to play. That's when I got introduced to the wonders of modern medicine. The doctors gave me a shot and the pain was miraculously gone. I started the game, threw four touchdowns in the first half and called it a night.

We won 58-3—LSU's worst beating in 100 years of playing intercollegiate football. This is an especially good memory for me now that I'm living in Louisiana surrounded by a rowdy bunch of Tiger fans.

DEVASTATING LOSS TO AUBURN

The next week we played against the Auburn Tigers. They went undefeated that year but couldn't play for the Southeastern Conference title because they were on NCAA probation. The game turned out to be a significant game in my development as a quarterback. But, unfortunately, for all the wrong reasons.

We started the game off on fire. I hit Jack Jackson for a long touchdown, we kicked a field goal, we were marching down the field at will and their crowd was not a factor. In fact, we gained 386 yards to their 104 in the first half. On our third drive, we were on Auburn's 4-yard line getting ready to score and take a 17-0 lead. If we had scored there, I really believe it would have broken their backs and made it nearly impossible for them to come back. Then Coach Spurrier signalled in what ended up being a play that haunts me still.

Earlier that week, Coach came up with an idea of running a quick flat-curl route on the goal line, which is a really strange pattern to attempt that close to the end zone. But you have to understand, Coach often came up with new and unique plays; he was constantly putting in things that were sometimes hard to visualize how they'd work in a game situation. The play may have seemed dangerous, but Coach assured us it would work against the right defensive coverage.

My experience as a quarterback was that you had to trust Coach Spurrier. He often came up with strategies that were hard to envision, but they always worked. It was unbelievable how they worked. Anyway, that whole week, although I really didn't see how this flat-curl could lead to anything but trouble, I made a concerted effort to drop my concerns and blindly follow directions. I'd do exactly as I was told. I wouldn't even think twice when he called it; I'd just run the play and trust Coach Spurrier.

Well, wouldn't you know it, when we got to Auburn's 4-yard line, he signalled in the short flat-curl. At least that is what I thought he signalled. Actually, it was a totally different play, a backside slant to Chris Doering. But the mind works in strange ways. I was so nervous he was going to call the flat-curl that's the signal I thought I saw. Although the signals were similar, I saw the wrong one and called the wrong play. The defender tripped Willie Jackson, knocking him over, and the Auburn cornerback intercepted my pass and ran 96 yards for a touchdown. Looking back on the tape, Chris Doering was one-on-one on the backside, and if I had called the right play, if I had read the signal correctly, there's a good chance Chris would have been open for a touchdown. So instead of being ahead 17-0, we were ahead only 10-7.

It's incredibly frustrating for me to know that my mistake, one simple miscommunication, could have cost us a huge victory. Later in the game, I went back and saw an open receiver way down the field. As I reared back to throw, I felt certain this would end up a touchdown. But I got hit as I was throwing, and that pass got intercepted, too, and returned 65 yards, all the way back to our 10-yard line. That's the type of game it was. Even though Errict Rhett ran for a career-high 196 yards and I threw for 386 yards and three touchdowns, every little thing fell into place for the Tigers, and they were able to kick a field goal at the end to win 38-35.

It was a significant game because I believe it gave Coach Spurrier the idea that he wanted Terry Dean to become the starting quarterback again.

BACK ON THE BENCH

We went to Jacksonville the next week for "the world's largest outdoor cocktail party," and right before the game, during warmups, the skies opened and we ended up in a typhoon. I remember going out and stepping in water that totally covered my shoes up to my socks. When the game started, it was still pouring and the field was a quagmire. It was an incredibly difficult environment to play in, and at one point early in the game, Coach Spurrier asked me if the rain was bothering me. I wasn't trying to make excuses—Coach hated excuses—but I answered his question honestly: "Yes." What else could I say? I mean, it is a lot harder to throw the ball in the pouring rain. Singing in the rain is a lot easier than slinging in the rain.

Well, a couple of things happened, I completed only three of my first nine passing attempts, and Coach Spurrier felt it was time to make a quarterback change. Terry Dean said at the time that he was looking for a dry spot on the bench when he heard Coach Spurrier yelling for him to get ready to go into the game.

"I'm thinking, 'Yeah, right,'" Terry told reporters after the game. "I'm thinking, 'Sure.' Coach Spurrier's told me before to get warm and then I didn't get in. To tell you the truth, I didn't think I'd ever play quarterback again at the University of Florida."

If I've learned anything over the years, it's never say never with Coach Spurrier. So he put Terry Dean back in the game, and Terry played well. Errict Rhett ran the ball like a man that day through the mud. He carried a school-record 41 times for 183 yards and we ended up winning 33-26.

After the game, Coach Spurrier made a change and decided that Terry would be starting again. "Terry is our quarterback," Coach Spurrier stated afterward. "Terry is going to start the next game. He's looked extremely good in practice, he's had a great attitude and he's back. Terry's back in the box."

And I was back on the bench…again. It was a very tough and frustrating time, but I understood the decision and tried to be very supportive. Terry had come into the game and provided a spark; he deserved to start, but one thing I learned during that Georgia game is that the old saying really is true—figuratively and literally: Into each life, a little rain must fall.

BATTLE OF WOUNDED KNEE

For the most part, Terry played out the rest of the season, although Coach Spurrier went back and forth between the two of us in the Vanderbilt game and actually started me against Florida State.

I played a decent first half against the Seminoles and it was a close game. But at the end of the first half, I dropped back, got hit and slightly twisted my right knee. It felt a little rubbery and loose, but I continued playing the rest of the half. At halftime, Dr. Pete (Pete Indelicato was our orthopaedic surgeon who still owes me a home-cooked Italian meal. Dr. Pete, if you're reading this: It's time to pay up) looked at my knee, and between the injury and the way the game was progressing, Coach Spurrier decided to put Terry in. After the game, Dr. Pete put me on crutches, which I thought was totally unnecessary; I was convinced I was fine. On Monday, I had an MRI and they found some damaged cartilage in my knee and a partially torn anterior cruciate ligament—the dreaded ACL. I had surgery two days later, and that was it for the rest of the season.

For the remainder of my college career, the knee held up very well, but I did decide to wear knee braces on both of my knees for extra protection. Once I left college, the knee slowly began to give me a little trouble, probably due to aging and the ongoing wear and tear of football. To this day, I have to be careful when I'm running on concrete or playing basketball; if I push it too hard, it swells up. But compared to many of my fellow football buddies, I made out quite well.

For the most part, I've really been blessed on the injury front. I had a long career in football, but I'm still very healthy and enjoy staying active. I look forward to playing with my son as he gets older. I know a lot of old football players can't even do that. They sacrificed their bodies for the game, and now they're paying the price.

My freshman season was filled with good times and frustrating times, but I think Terry and I both learned something that might best be epitomized by a poster Terry used to have hanging in his locker. The poster showed a pelican swallowing a frog. The frog was going down the pelican's throat headfirst, but his legs dangled out of the mouth and clutched tightly around the pelican's throat, preventing the pelican from swallowing him. The caption under the picture read: "Don't Ever Give Up."

4

GAME PREP: WHAT IT TAKES TO BE A GATOR

GETTING TUTENIZED

I n high school, I always strived to be the hardest worker on my team. Whether it was gruelling runs in the heat and humidity of a Florida summer or the grind of the winter weightlifting program, I wanted to get the most out of my body. I was a dedicated, self-motivated athlete. But still, when I arrived at UF, and in particular when I started my first off-season workout program in January of 1993, my eyes were opened to what "getting in shape" really meant.

After my first season, Coach Spurrier brought in Rich Tuten to direct the strength and conditioning program, and his name is both famous and infamous among Gator athletes from several eras. Coach Tuten was at UF in the early 1980s and returned with a tough-guy, drill-sergeant reputation that preceded him. We knew he was serious when he showed up after the bowl game of my freshman season (the Gator Bowl) and told us we had two days off before the off-season conditioning program started. Two days? Wow, thanks for the break, big guy.

GETTING A LEG UP

Coach Tuten was a big believer in the leg press exercise. He believed the leg press machine was a great way to build strength, endurance, and mental toughness. When I showed up for my first workout, Coach Tuten wanted me to do 350 pounds on the leg press, which was no problem—except he wanted me to do it 12 TIMES! There had to be a mistake. He must have been reading my chart wrong. My one-rep max was only 500 pounds. Nobody tells you to do 70 percent of your max weight on the leg press 12 times. Nobody except Rich Tuten. I got on the machine and pressed the first rep up, then the second one, then I strained REALLY HARD to get the third one, and I barely squeaked out the fourth. I knew there was no way I could do another one. I felt if I could get just half of the fifth rep, that would impress him, so I fought it and somehow, some way, I grunted and groaned and managed to get the fifth one up. And I knew for sure that was it; I was done. And then I heard that lovely voice that I would hear so many times over the next few years. It was Coach Tuten screaming: "SEVEN MORE!" He helped me a little bit, which he would do as long as you were pushing as hard as you possibly could, but it seemed like I was there for hours trying to get to 12.

It was one of the most excruciatingly miserable moments of my life. Several players either fell out or vomited trying to get to 12. We actually had trashcans next to the leg press machine where guys could just lean over and throw up—and then go right on lifting. It was brutal. But that was Coach Tuten. He worked you to a point where you thought you couldn't do any more, and then somehow pushed you to press on.

It was sheer agony at the time, but looking back at it, that was the strongest I've ever been. On the bench press, I was able to do 225 pounds 19 times, which equates out to about a 365-

pound max. That's pretty darn good for a quarterback. In fact, Coach Spurrier thought the quarterbacks worked out too hard and too long under Coach Tuten. Coach Spurrier grew up in an era when heavy weightlifting was more for the big linemen, not the skill-position players. He believed too much weightlifting made a quarterback stiff and robotic. He was right to a point, but we still had to sneak our heavy lifting in while Coach Spurrier wasn't around. I remember once, we had 225 pounds on the squat bar, which was just a light weight we would warm up with. That's when Coach Spurrier walked in and nearly had a fit when he saw I had 225 pounds on my back. "Danny, what are you doing with that much weight?" he said. "You need to put about half that on there, just enough to loosen you up; that's all you need." Thank goodness he didn't come in 10 minutes later when we put the real weight on the bar.

Not only did we do weightlifting during the off-season, we had 6:30 a.m. conditioning runs—long-distance runs, timed sprints, and agility drills. One summer, on the first day of training, one of our freshman linebackers spent all night drinking and partying, and he came straight to the workout. I guess he didn't have a clue what to expect. We were outside in the sun with chains strapped to our waists pulling heavy sleds around the practice field. This freshman, who shall remain anonymous, experienced one of the worst mornings of his life. However, he was such a great athlete I think he still pulled the sled faster and farther than I did.

From reading this, it might seem like they overworked us, but that's the commitment you have to put forth if you want to become a champion. When I think back on those times now, I really appreciate what great strength and conditioning coaches we had at Florida. After going through that regimen, I truly felt like I could run through walls. The human body supposedly can't do certain things, but we did them anyway. It was total mastery over your body—mind over matter. The toughness we developed was incredible. Coach Tuten was a tough coach, but in the end all the hard work paid huge dividends.

After Coach Tuten moved on to the NFL, Coach Spurrier hired Jerry Schmidt from Notre Dame as the head strength coach, and he brought Rob Glass to help direct the program. We hoped this new regime would offer a lighter burden than its predecessor, but the program proved to be every bit as demanding and intense as Coach Tuten's. While the speed and weight training was of a slightly different variety—there was a strong focus on explosiveness and position specific training—we didn't get any relief.

As I reflect on my entire career at UF, I have no doubt the quality strength and conditioning programs helped us win the four Southeastern Conference championships and the national title. And after comparing college programs with other NFL athletes during my seven years in the league, I'm certain we were trained by the best in the business while at the University of Florida.

GAME WEEK

Monday: Game week started for the Gators on Monday. We'd usually get a couple of weightlifting sessions in each week, and one of them was traditionally on Monday. But we did something unique at the University of Florida, something that was different than just about every other school: We had "Monday night football." And, no, we're not talking about John Madden and Al Michaels's *Monday Night Football*.

Here's how our Monday night football worked: We'd meet later in the day than normal, usually around 4 o'clock or so. We'd watch the tape of the previous game and the coaches would make corrections; then they'd make some positive (and

I'm putting on my intense game face while stretching. This is when you're supposed to look real tough before a game and intimidate your opponent or at least convince your coach you mean business. *(Andy Lyons/Getty Images)*

sometimes negative) comments about our performance the week before. Then, we'd go eat an early dinner in the dining hall, come back for more meetings and then go out on the practice field and have Monday night football.

Monday night football was basically a special-teams practice at the beginning, followed by the coaching staff giving us some initial thoughts and ideas about the week ahead. But the highlight was the second half of practice, which was a scrimmage for the younger players who rarely played on Saturday. Early in my career, Monday night football proved to be instrumental in my development as a QB.

Long before I ever threw the famous touchdown pass to Chris Doering against Kentucky, the two of us were playing pitch and catch during Monday night football. I remember throwing my first touchdown pass during one of those Monday night practices, and what a confidence boost that was for me. Young players often feel left out, like they're not really that much a part of the team. Monday night football was a great way to give those guys a chance to show the coaches what they could do.

Tuesday and Wednesday: Tuesday was the day the real grunt work started. Practices were longer and more intense on Tuesday and Wednesdays than any other day of the week. We'd start with a very long individual period. This is when the team would split up and each coach would work with his particular position group. The amount of time the quarterbacks got to work with Coach Spurrier on techniques and fundamentals was phenomenal. A lot of teams ran similar plays to ours, but the attention to detail—like, for instance, your head position on certain passing plays—is what separated Coach Spurrier. He was very particular and picky about teaching things like that. And during individual drills, Coach Spurrier would be with the quarterbacks the entire time. Many head coaches walk around and let the assistants do the dirty work. Not Coach Spurrier.

He'd be right there the entire practice, coaching the quarterbacks every second and often grabbing a football to show us exactly how he wanted it done.

After individual drills, we'd move into some group-type work, where we would have running drills, seven-on-seven drills, interior line drills and so forth. Then we'd do our specialized running game and passing game drills, followed by full squad drills and, finally, conditioning. We'd usually wrap everything up around 6 o'clock.

The schedule was much the same on Wednesday—more meetings and another long practice. No question about it, Tuesday and Wednesday were the toughest days of the week.

Thursday: By the time Thursday rolled around, the coaches began to back off and lighten things up from a physical perspective. You don't want heavy legs for the game, and Coach Spurrier never wanted his players getting hurt in practice. That could easily happen if you hit too much late in the week. Mainly, Thursday was for tuning up the special teams and running through our key plays.

Friday: On Fridays, we'd meet in the afternoon around 4 o'clock, and if it was a home game, we'd have a walk-through in the Swamp. We'd have some slight warm-up drills, the receivers and quarterbacks would run through some plays and the linemen would play a walking touch football game. It was part of their pregame ritual.

PRACTICE MAKES PERFECT

Chris Doering and I used to have our own pregame ritual right after the walk-through on Friday, and it paid off. We went into the red zone—I'd be around the 15-yard line and Chris would run across the back of the end zone. We'd practice a situation where Chris would have a bunch of guys around him

I'm getting some last-minute coaching before a game.
(Photo courtesy of Florida Sports Information)

and I'd throw the ball to a spot—about 10 feet high near the goalpost in the back of the endzone. He'd then leap up as high as he could, snatch the ball out of the air and try to land with his feet in bounds. For years, we practiced that situation at every Friday walk-through.

One of my most memorable and exciting plays at the University of Florida was my junior year against South Carolina in Columbia. It was a cold, windy night, and, sure enough, Chris and I found ourselves in a very familiar situation. I was on about the 15- or 20-yard line when I went back to pass and got flushed from the pocket to my right. I was scrambling for my life, defenders were chasing me and all I could see was this mass of jerseys—both Gators and Gamecocks—in the back of the end zone. And—yeah, you guessed it—right behind that mass of jerseys, I saw Chris "streaking" across the back line. I knew what he was thinking; he knew what I was thinking. Without any hesitation, I pretended like I didn't see anybody else out there except Chris. I just aimed for our spot and let go of the pass. It was almost like slow motion. The ball arrived and everybody went up, but Chris knew exactly where the ball would be and knew exactly when to jump. His timing was perfect. He grabbed the ball out of the air, came down and landed with one foot in bounds. Touchdown, Gators! It's a beautiful thing when one's creativity, dedication, and practice come together and payoff. And it's all the more special when it happens with a great friend like Chris Doering.

MEALS AND MOVIES

After the Friday walk-through, we'd either take a bus to the airport and fly to the opponent's city or, if it was a home game, we'd bus over to the Holiday Inn on the west side of Gainesville. We'd check into the hotel, and go right to the pregame meal.

Let me tell you something about our pregame meals: They were always special, always good ... and always the same. You could count on every Friday night having chicken, lasagne, macaroni and cheese, mashed potatoes and green beans. That was Coach Spurrier's menu. In fact, when I was in the NFL and played for Coach Spurrier with the Redskins, we had exactly the same menu. You had to be creative with the A-1 or Heinz 57 to try to spice things up. Have you ever had A-1 on macaroni and cheese? Not bad. Not bad at all.

One part of the pregame experience I always liked at UF was the Friday night movies. The coaches would take the entire team to a theater so we could watch a movie the night before the game. It was a way for us to escape and get football off our minds for a while. We always looked forward to it. There were several memorable movies that we saw, but what was even more memorable was watching the linemen go to the concession area and come back with their barrels of buttered popcorn. One time, offensive lineman Anthony Ingrassia was sitting beside me at the theater. He came in with his popcorn, went to sit in his chair, and the chair actually broke off and landed on the floor. Yes, Anthony was a big man—a very big man.

After the movie, we'd always go back to the hotel and have a team snack. I was told that before Coach Spurrier became the coach at UF, the team snack would be Wendy's cheeseburgers, which was a treat all the guys loved and looked forward to. Well, when Coach Spurrier became the coach, it was switched to turkey sandwiches and celery sticks. He continued to be very health conscious, which was frustrating at the time, but now that I'm older I appreciate what he was trying to do.

CATCHING UP

After the snack, all the players would go back to our rooms and check in. Chris Doering was my roommate on the road until he graduated a year ahead of me. In the hotel room, we would always have a football catching contest. We'd toss a football back and forth pretty hard and see who would be the first to drop it. He may not admit this now, but I won almost every time. I'd joke with him that the quarterback of the team had better hands than he did.

People often ask why the Gators stay at a hotel for home games; why not just stay on campus and save the money? Personally, I think the hotel is a great idea. The city of Gainesville starts crawling with people on Fridays before home games. There are fans coming from all directions and there are many distractions—especially for college guys. It would simply be too difficult to stay focused, and who knows what could have happened if players were spread out all over town in their own apartments. Plus, I liked it because our hotel in Gainesville— the Holiday Inn West—held fond memories for me. That was the same place my high school team stayed when we won the state championship at Florida Field.

GAME DAY AT LAST

On game-day mornings, we'd wake up and have our pregame meal. We'd always eat exactly four hours prior to kickoff, which is pretty standard for most teams. The logic is that four hours is just the right amount of time to get hydrated and get energy in your body without having the food laying on your stomach and bothering you throughout the game. After eating, we'd go back to the room usually for about 15 or 20 minutes before the buses left, and that was a special time for Chris and me. Chris, like many of the guys on the team, would listen to music during this time. One of the songs he always listened to was a classical song—Pachelbel's "Canon in D." It was a song I always liked, too, so we started a ritual: He would listen to it and then hand me the headphones and I would listen to it. Then we'd say a prayer and head for the bus. One of my favorite articles any sportswriter ever wrote at Florida was entitled "Classic Connection." It was about the chemistry Chris and I had on and off the field and the affinity we both had for classical music.

The bus ride to the game was always a special time. We had offensive and defensive buses, and I, of course, was on the offensive bus with Coach Spurrier. He always liked it quiet and had the mindset that this was a serious time and there should be no joking around. I can still hear him saying, "No laughing and giggling." I heard the defensive bus with James Bates and Co. was little rowdier. At home games, we'd get on Interstate 75, go South, turn off on Archer Road and wind our way back toward campus. What a scene. It really was like the parting of the Red Sea when the buses would come through campus. All of the loyal and passionate fans were incredible. It was amazing to see their reactions—the thumbs up, the cheers, all the yelling.

We'd pull into the stadium at the south end zone and many of the players' parents would be there to greet us. My mom used to tell me that she thought there was something wrong with me as I would step off the bus. She said I was so serious and stone-faced that I looked like a zombie, like I was living in another world. I guess you could say I had my game face on. With all the pressure, intensity and concentration required to run Coach Spurrier's offense, I always found that it worked best if I had a really serious, focused mind-set as we got ready for the game.

We'd always walk around the field to try to get a feel for the conditions. I think that tradition dates back to the old days when the fields had holes, bumps and wet spots in them, and it really behooved you to scout them out beforehand. It's really not all that necessary these days, but tradition is tradition.

After walking the field, we'd go into the locker room, get dressed and taped and then head out for warm-ups. The warm-up period was always the worst for me. I'm just not a good warm-up type of guy. I remember Coach Spurrier used to always say, "If you watched Danny Wuerffel in warm-ups, you'd think he couldn't play a lick." It was true, too. There was always somebody on our team who looked like a better QB than I did during warm-ups.

After warm-ups was the time when we'd go back in the locker room and Coach Spurrier would go around to every player and greet them, tell them good luck and shake hands. I saw a documentary once where Coach Spurrier was coaching the USFL Tampa Bay Bandits back in the early 1980s and, sure enough, that was his pregame ritual back then, too. But he did kind of change up the ritual in recent years. Instead of shaking hands, he'd do the trendy thing and make a fist and tap it on top of your fist. Well, I say it was the trendy thing, but knowing how health conscious Coach Spurrier is, I wonder if he did it because he didn't want to shake hands and get all those germs.

A lot of coaches will try to motivate you right before the game with fiery pregame speeches, but that wasn't Coach Spurrier's style. He thought that the motivation should come during the week and should come from within. While you may indeed get fired up for the pregame speech, that feeling lasts only until the opening kickoff, and then you're back to relying on internal motivation. I couldn't agree more with his philosophy. Something Coach Spurrier said over and over: "If something good happens, keep playing. If something bad happens, keep playing."

TUNNELING IN

Just before making our way out onto the field for the game, we'd always get in a circle and say The Lord's Prayer together. Right after that, you could sense the excitement, and some guys even worked themselves into a frenzy. I always had to be careful during this time. An overzealous head butt in pregame could easily cause as much damage as a blitzing linebacker. I thought it was always a good idea to keep some distance.

There's a big Gator head right outside our locker room at the entrance to the field, and we'd all touch it before running through the tunnel that came out of the south end zone.

Coming out of that tunnel is one of the most surreal things you can imagine. The first time I ever ran through it and onto Florida Field, it was like I had entered another world, another dimension, where reality ended and a cartoon-like universe began. You become awash in color and noise. All around you, beneath you, beside you and above you, you can feel the force of the deafening crowd. It's an amazing sensation, it really is. You can actually feel the fans—their passion, their loyalty, their strength and their wills—lifting you up. I think without a doubt, the Swamp is one of the greatest—if not the greatest environment—in all of college football.

SWIMMING IN THE SWAMP

We didn't lose many games at the Swamp during my five seasons in Gainesville. In fact, I think we were 29-2 at home during that time. I really got a chance to observe what a tremendous advantage it is to play at Florida Field during my redshirt freshman season when I stood on the sideline and wasn't playing. That's when you can really experience the atmosphere and actually feel the crowd. As I got older and started playing, I couldn't allow myself to get caught up in the excitement of the game because I had to stay focused and attuned to the thought process of each play.

When I look back on it, the home-field advantage at the Swamp can be compared to two swimmers—one swimming downstream in a current and the other swimming in calm water. The swimmers both might work just as hard and use the same amount of energy, but the swimmer going with the current is moving so much faster. He may not notice how fast he's going, but the current is carrying him along. I think that would explain my experience with the tremendous crowd support at the Swamp: Although I wasn't always focused on it, it undeniably carried me and our team along.

I loved leading the mighty Gators down the field.
(Scott Halleran/Getty Images)

PRAYING AND SINGING

There were a couple of postgame traditions that I always enjoyed at UF. After the battles and intense competition from the game, I particularly enjoyed meeting and praying at midfield with members of both teams. This provided a great opportunity to stay connected with other players who knew that some things were more important than winning and losing.

Following the prayer, our opponents would go to their locker room—usually dejected from another loss at the Swamp—and our entire team would turn, face the band, and sing our alma, which is a tradition Coach Spurrier brought back to the Swamp. That was an interesting experience, especially to the younger players. Few of us knew the words at first so they had to put them up on the scoreboard so we could sing along.

AUTOGRAPHS, AUTOGRAPHS, AND MORE AUTOGRAPHS

At home games, after meeting with the media for postgame interviews, I'd always try to leave the locker room via a door by the south end zone. But as we would come out of the door, there were usually hundreds, if not thousands, of fans waiting to get autographs. Early in my career, I'd sign a few autographs and leave with my dad. No problem. But as I got older, there would be more and more people and crowd maintenance became an issue. We ended up having some police officers on hand to keep things from getting out of control. It actually got to a point where a lot of players were exiting through other doors to try to avoid the crowd. I was always tempted to do that, and, looking back, maybe I should have for my own benefit. But I just always felt an obligation to go out and spend a little bit of time connecting with the fans. Sometimes, though, that little bit of time turned into two hours.

One of my most memorable autograph sessions came after one home game when I was at a small community outside of Gainesville eating dinner. It wasn't unusual for people to approach me during a meal and ask for an autograph, but this time we'd just won a big game and there were a whole lot of excited Gators. After several interruptions to our dinner, the owner came up to me and said sympathetically, "Danny, what would you like me to do?" I told him I'd stay after dinner as long as it took if he would just let us finish our meal. So the owner went out and spread the word, and you wouldn't believe it. In the time it took for us to eat our meal, apparently the word spread throughout the entire community. When I stepped outside the restaurant, there was a line of people all the way down the block and I ended up staying for hours signing autographs and having pictures taken.

POSTGAME PANIC
AT 30,000 FEET

After the away games we would shower up, head right to the airport and fly home. I tell a lot of people that in the course my football career, I've been to many cities all around the country, but I've only seen the stadiums, airports, and hotels. One particularly memorable road trip came during my redshirt year when we were coming home after playing Tennessee. We'd just got beaten badly, 31-14, and we were really frustrated. But the trip got much more bizarre and scary as we were flying along about 30,000 feet over parts unknown.

What actually happened was the cabin pressure dropped inside the plane, which meant the oxygen level was getting so low that it was difficult to breathe. This is not terribly uncommon, but we didn't know what was going on at the time. When the oxygen level drops in a plane, the pilot makes an emergency descent from 30,000 feet to 10,000 feet so you can resume breathing normally again. But, again, we didn't know any of the specifics or logistics of what was happening.

All we knew is that we were riding along at 30,000 feet, dinner had just been served and we were really hungry. When the flight attendants finally brought our food, you could feel this strange popping sensation in your ears. And then the oxygen masks popped down from above. And then the plane took a nosedive.

Nobody told us this was an emergency descent. For all we knew, this was a death dive. And no one said anything. Even the flight attendants were scared and nervous. It's not a good thing when the people you're supposed to trust look worried. As for me, maybe I'm naïve, but my food had just been brought to me and I was hungry, so I tried to continue eating as we made our descent. While I was getting oxygen from the mask, I'd take breaks periodically to take a few bites of food. I also remember reaching up and putting my hand on the shoulder of Jason Odom, who was sitting in front of me. It was my way of letting him know everything would be OK. But he told me later that it didn't calm him down at all. In fact, he said he was doing fine until I put my hand on his shoulder. He thought it was my way of saying, "I love you and I'll see you in heaven."

As we were making our "emergency descent," I'm told that some of the boosters who were on the plane with the administration were so scared that they … well, let me put this way, some undergarments needed to be cleaned when the plane landed.

As it turned out, we didn't crash and all turned out well. Everybody got over it except defensive tackle Ellis Johnson. From that point on, he refused to take the team plane on road trips and would actually ride out a couple of days early on the equipment truck.

5

QB QUANDARY: MY SOPHOMORE SEASON

TERRY WINS THE JOB

At the end of my freshman season, Terry Dean was named the Most Valuable Player in the Southeastern Conference Championship game against Alabama, and then led us to a 41-7 blow out of West Virginia in the Sugar Bowl.

Terry did a great job at the end of that season and, of course, I was out with a knee injury. The following spring, Coach Spurrier publicly announced that the quarterback position was open and that we would be having a competition during spring drills and fall training camp to see who'd be the starter.

Personally, I really didn't feel it was a wide-open competition. Even though Terry and I were competing, I could sense from the beginning that Coach Spurrier was leaning toward Terry. And, believe it or not, I thought it was the right thing to do, because Terry was going to be a senior and had earned the job at the end of the previous season. The year before had been a topsy-turvy, back-and-forth season between the two of us, and Terry ended up on top. I was very understanding of that and supported Coach Spurrier's decision to start off with Terry in 1994, even though it was tough.

TERRY GOES ON A TEAR

Terry started the season on fire. Everything was going just right. We were the preseason No. 1-ranked team in the country and Terry was being mentioned as a Heisman Trophy candidate. In the first game of the season, we beat New Mexico State 70-21, and Terry threw an incredible seven touchdown passes. Sometimes, we all get numb to the numbers our offense put up at Florida, but to get an idea of how astounding those seven touchdown passes were that afternoon, consider this: No other Southeastern Conference quarterback had ever thrown even six touchdown passes in a game before, and Terry had six with 34 minutes still left to play. His seventh tied the NCAA record set a quarter-century earlier by San Diego State's Dennis Shaw. Coach Spurrier said after the opener that, "Terry has as much talent as any quarterback I've ever coached. He could potentially be one of the best to ever play here."

From there, we continued to blow out everybody. We beat Kentucky 73-7; we shut out Tennessee 31-0; we routed Ole Miss and LSU by a combined score of 80-32. But even though we were winning, Coach Spurrier is a perfectionist and wasn't entirely happy with the way Terry was playing. So even though the Heisman talk was running rampant in the media, Coach Spurrier was having some second thoughts in his mind about Terry.

Terry knew it, too. He would tell author Peter Golenbock later: "After the LSU game, I knew I was in trouble. It's hard to describe it...but I knew I was on thin ice."

One thing I've always admired about Coach Spurrier was that he didn't just care about the statistics or the final score. He coached us to do certain things, and he evaluated us based on how well we followed his instructions. I know that during my career, I had some phenomenal games statistically where I actually didn't play so well—my mistakes just didn't happen to be very costly. Some of my best performances actually came with lesser stats. Sometimes, stats are based on other factors, like who was the opponent or how well your teammates played. An effective coach looks at all the factors to evaluate a player's performance, and the fans and media aren't always privy to what's really happening.

ANOTHER MELTDOWN AGAINST AUBURN

We were 5-0 and atop the polls heading into Auburn. It was a huge game for us because Auburn had beaten us the year before on a last-second field goal (remember the whole signal blunder ordeal?... I sure do). This time, the game was at Florida Field and the hype was enormous. The media was calling it "Super Saturday" or the "Southern Super Bowl" or some other catchy moniker that tried to capture the importance of the game.

Terry did not have a good game. He seemed to be having trouble with Auburn's seven-man zones and threw four interceptions in the first half. I entered the game in the second half and played pretty well. I completed 10 of 13 passes for 171 yards and three touchdowns. However, we lost the game again in the final seconds when Auburn's Frank Sanders caught a touchdown pass from Patrick Nix with just eight seconds left to give the Tigers a 36-33 victory.

I'm enjoying a little Gatorade between drives in the Florida sun—surely everyone knows that Gatorade was invented at the University of Florida. Is it in you? *(Photo courtesy of Florida Sports Information)*

After the Auburn game, Terry was as frustrated as a quarterback could be and said some things to the media he probably shouldn't have said. One thing Coach Spurrier never liked was a player airing out his problems in the newspapers.

"When he took me out, I was kind of surprised. But when you think about what he said to me this week, I guess I shouldn't have been," Terry told the media in the locker room after the game. "He's the head coach and he can do whatever he wants. I guess now I'll just sit on the bench like last year and hope I get another opportunity."

He never did. It was an emotional time and a devastating loss, and it would be the end of Terry's career as a quarterback at the University of Florida. After that game, Coach Spurrier announced that I would be the starter for the remainder of the season.

MY RELATIONSHIP
WITH TERRY

Some people thought Terry and I didn't like each other, but that wasn't the case at all. I always felt the two of us had a really good relationship. A lot of times, when people are competing for the same position, there's a mind-set that you shouldn't be getting along. My perspective was always that, yes, I was competing against Terry, but it really wasn't up to him or me; it was up to Coach Spurrier. So, there was no reason whatsoever for me to dislike Terry. In fact, I was very sympathetic for the frustrations he went through, and if I were in his shoes, I would have been frustrated with a lot of things, too.

Terry and I always got along really well and I think we handled the situation as cordially as could be expected. I tried to be supportive of him and I think he tried to be supportive of me, too. Even after Terry and I left UF, we stayed in touch. He did a football camp in his hometown of Naples a few years ago, and I went down to help. After the camp, we both spoke at his church. It was good to see Terry again and talk about some of the old times.

Being a quarterback is tough duty, even if you're the backup. You're obviously cheering hard for your team to win, but you're also competitive and want to be playing. Believe me, I've been in a lot of different quarterback "situations" in college and in the NFL, and my philosophy was to not only root for the team, but to root for the quarterback who was out there playing. I'll be honest, there's always a little voice in your head that hopes the other guy doesn't do well so you can get a chance to play. That's human nature. Part of my faith, I believe, allowed me to take those negative thoughts captive and not allow them to grow. This enabled the pure things and the pure thoughts to take over. I'd be lying if I said my thoughts were always incredibly supportive of the other guy. Sometimes, negative thoughts do creep in. But one thing I can say: I tried my best to quash that detrimental line of thinking so I could be respectful and supportive of the quarterbacks who were playing ahead of me.

POOPING AND PUKING

Later that year, we travelled to Nashville to play Vanderbilt, and the game was memorable for one reason: I got unbelievably sick. I vomited and had diarrhea the entire night before the game. The trainers kept telling me to drink, drink, and drink some more to avoid getting dehydrated. And I remember Coach Spurrier telling backup quarterback Eric Kresser, "Get ready, Eric, because Danny is pooping and puking. You might get in there."

I looked so sick before the game that when I went to get on the team bus, Terry Dean jokingly pulled his warm-up jacket up over his face to avoid contamination. I remember going out for the game, and I was so drained that all I could think about was wanting to sleep. At any point during the game, I think I could have laid on the sideline and took a nap. Certainly, the Vandy fans wouldn't have disturbed me.

But I wasn't about to sit out the game. No way. I had finally won the starting job and I wasn't going to leave the door open for somebody else.

It's amazing what the human body can do when adrenaline kicks in. Once I got on the field and into the flow of the game, I ended up completing 18 of 23 passes and we won 24-7. That set up two huge games at the end of the season—one for the state championship and the other for the conference championship.

I was always dedicated to warming up for a big game.
(Photo courtesy of Florida Sports Information)

CHOKE AT DOAK

I've seen some comebacks in my career, but unfortunately the most amazing one came when we jumped ahead of Florida State 31-3 at Doak Campbell Stadium. Everyone thought the game was in hand, but we somehow let it slip out of our grasp. Who would have ever guessed going into the fourth quarter that they would be able to pull it out? Football is such a crazy game. So many things had to happen just right for them to come back from such a deficit—and everything did.

Bobby Bowden was actually considering doing a Steve Spurrier impersonation and pulling quarterback Danny Kanell out of the game in the third quarter when the FSU fans were chanting "Busby! Busby!" in honor of backup quarterback Thad

Busby. But Coach Bowden stuck with Kanell, which turned out to be one of the best decisions he's ever made.

Kanell went 18 for 22 for 232 yards—and that was just in the fourth quarter! The Seminoles scored four touchdowns in that final quarter to tie the record for greatest fourth-quarter comeback in NCAA history. Even though the game ended in a 31-31 tie, it certainly felt like a loss to us.

After the game, some of our defensive players publicly questioned our defensive coaches for playing such soft coverages in the fourth quarter. You know the old saying: "The only thing the prevent defense does is prevent you from winning." Second-guessing the coaches is probably not a healthy reaction, but it sort of epitomized the incredible frustration we all felt that day. The next morning in the *Gainesville Sun*, some smart-aleck columnist named Mike Bianchi called our performance "The Choke at Doak." It was a game none of us are proud of and will definitely go down in the annals as one of the lowlights of my career. I'm still looking for that Bianchi guy to give him a piece of my mind.

MY FIRST SEC CHAMPIONSHIP AS A STARTER

In my freshman year, we won the SEC title, but I was injured at the time and Terry was our starting quarterback. It's hard to feel like part of the team when you're standing on the sideline with crutches watching everyone else play. But going to Atlanta for the SEC Championship Game during my sophomore season was quite a thrill. I was the starter and we were playing undefeated Alabama, which had one of the top defenses in the country. This game, along with the Kentucky game during my freshman season, stands out as two of the most memorable of my career.

Coach Spurrier always met with the media on Tuesdays of game week, and on this particular Tuesday he turned to several Alabama writers with a message for Crimson Tide defensive coordinator "Brother" Bill Oliver.

"You guys go tell Brother Bill I've got some new ball plays for him," Coach said.

He wasn't kidding either. We pulled out all the stops that day against Alabama's vaunted defense. We threw the old Emory & Henry formation at them (more info to follow), we ran a double pass, a quarterback sneak that became a slant pass and we even used a bit of deception.

WINNING A CHAMPIONSHIP

Unlike the week before against Florida State, this time it was our turn to come from behind. Alabama was really playing well and, as always back then, the Tide defense never gave away anything without a fight. Near the end of the game, I threw a pass that ended up getting tipped, intercepted and returned for a touchdown. We were behind by six points, and all the Alabama fans in the Georgia Dome were going crazy.

We had one drive left to win the game, and we had 80 yards to go against an incredibly good defense. We had a lot of wacky plays on that drive, but the key one was a play we'd been working on all week in practice. It was a play where I looked over to the sideline to see if (backup quarterback) Eric Kresser had his helmet on. If he did, that was a signal for me to hobble to the sidelines as if I were injured.

Sure enough, I looked over and Eric had his helmet on so I limped off the field like John Wayne in the Sands of Iwo Jima. It was perhaps my finest acting job since I played a majestic king in my third-grade play.

The strategy behind the play was to make Alabama relax a little bit. It's human nature to think that when a backup quarterback comes into the game, he's probably going to be a little timid. The defense is expecting you to play it safe and just run the ball, especially on the first play. This mentality, of course, draws the defense closer to the line of scrimmage and makes it easier to throw it deep.

Eric was a quarterback who had a cannon for an arm, and the plan all along was for me to hobble off the field so Eric could come in and fire it deep. Not only did Eric have a great arm, he had this uncanny ability to throw it as far as he could without warming up. On the first and only play Eric was in the game, he threw it 25 yards to Ike Hilliard to give us great field position at Alabama's 42-yard line. I then trotted back on the field "as good as new" to continue the drive.

I later found out that after the pass, Coach Spurrier began thinking about leaving Eric in to finish the game. Boy, am I glad I ran back on the field before Coach had time to finish that thought.

When I think back on it now, it's pretty interesting, because if Eric had finished that game and won it, who knows what would have happened the following season. Might there have been another quarterback controversy? You just never know what could have happened.

Many reporters have said that one of the reasons I flourished in Coach's system is because I could understand what he was thinking—what he really was trying to accomplish. I guess in that particular case, I was very fortunate to be oblivious to Coach's thoughts. Running back into the game without being told might have saved my job.

Another thing about that play: A few days after the game, I received a really nasty letter from a fan—probably an Alabama fan—who thought the play was deceptive and meant to purposely fool the defense. He felt the play was immoral—a

I'm concentrating on trying to hit an open receiver downfield.
(Photo courtesy of Florida Sports Information)

"chink in my character armor." I'd never really thought about it before, because I've always felt that much of the game of football is about deceiving the defense with play-action passes and all sorts of different fakes and gimmicks. I felt this play wasn't really any different.

One thing's for sure, we used every bit of trickery and deception we could on that final drive. After Eric's pass, we lined up in what we called the Emory & Henry set—an unconventional formation where the big offensive tackles actually line up wide next to the receivers. Most people have never seen anything like it, and the hope is the defense hasn't either. Before they can figure out how to get set, we'd hurry up to the line and run a play. We often used it in games just to keep a defense off balance and spark some momentum if we ever needed it. We sure needed it then, and we sure got it.

I threw a pass to Reidel Anthony, who nearly broke it for a touchdown. We lined up in it again and we ran a double pass—I threw a pass to Chris Doering, who then threw it 20 yards to Aubrey Hill getting us down to the Alabama 2. And, finally, as we lined up on the goal line for a quarterback sneak, I called an audible and hit Chris Doering on a quick, little two-yard slant for the winning touchdown and a 24-23 victory.

It was one of the most emotional games of my football career. Being able to come from behind and win a championship in such a pressurized situation was a phenomenal feeling. After the game, Coach Spurrier came up to me and gave me a huge hug. And as he did, I didn't think about it or plan it, I just blurted out, "Coach, I love you." It was really just a heartfelt expression of joy during a wonderful moment.

REDEAUX ON THE BAYOU

We played Florida State again in the Sugar Bowl that year, which seemed appropriate since the regular-season game ended in a 31-31 tie. The game was billed as "The Fifth Quarter in the French Quarter" and it was one of the most physical games I've ever played in.

Because the rivalry was so heated, there was a concern that violence might break out among Florida and Florida State players during Sugar Bowl week. Unfortunately for us, the fighting was among our own players. Two of our linebackers—

Darren Hambrick and Anthony Riggins—were sent home from New Orleans following a rather nasty fight during a Sugar Bowl dinner on the Saturday night before the game. Anthony, we heard later, actually had to go to the hospital to get stitches in his face.

Coach Spurrier was very embarrassed by the incident, and it certainly wasn't something you like to have happen before a big game. Following the incident, we went about our regular schedule of events and went to a movie.

"We saw *Dumb and Dumber*," defensive coordinator Bobby Pruett pointed out later. "How apropos."

The game itself was incredibly intense and hard-hitting— like all the FSU games. I was as banged up after that game as I've ever been in my life. When the game ended, I remember it being about a month before my body was back to normal. I was playing tennis the next February and still had a difficult time bending over to pick up a ball because my muscles ached and my back was still stiff.

A big deal was made during my senior season about Florida State's defense hitting me late, but the hardest hit I ever took in college came during that 1995 Sugar Bowl. I threw a slant pass to Jacquez Green and I actually saw him catch the ball—and that's when I got hit under the chin, lifted up into the air and dropped with a thud on the turf of the Super Dome (which at the time was just a little layer of artificial turf over a huge concrete slab). None of the hits I ever took my senior year were as rough (or as late) as that particular one. I don't know who it was who hit me, but he sure has a good clip for his highlight film.

The Seminoles won that particular "Redeaux on the Bayou," but as we all know, the Gators would win a much bigger, more important rematch in New Orleans two years later.

6

FRIENDS AND FOES: THE PERSONALITIES

One of the greatest aspects of playing football is the opportunity to meet so many unique and amazing people. One football team can have guys from the beach and the mountains, the north and the south. You can have both country rednecks and fellas from the inner city—players from all walks of life. Football provides one of the few arenas where men from drastically different cultures with different personalities unite for a common purpose. Some say a football team is one of the few truly integrated groups in American society. And in being part of such a team, you develop some phenomenal relationships.

Here are some of the important people who made an impact on my athletic career and some of the memorable personalities I played with and against at the University of Florida.

My high school coach, Jimmy Ray Stephens, and left tackle Larry Fleming join me for a photo after the UF/FSU game. Larry defected and went to the other school, but somehow we remained friends.

JIMMY RAY STEPHENS

During my seven years in the NFL, I often asked players to tell me about the most influential people in their lives. In almost every case, their high school football coach topped the list; I'm no exception.

I would be remiss to write a book about my football career and not start with the impact Jimmy Ray Stephens has had on my life. So much of who I am as a football player and a person, I owe to Coach Stephens, who was my head coach in high school and went on to become the Gators' offensive line coach during my years at UF.

I'll never forget the day he drove into Fort Walton Beach in a red Nissan Maxima; a day that would radically affect the course of my life in many ways. I couldn't possibly share all my great memories of Coach Stephens, but I'll never forget the

Here I am with five of the former Davey O'Brien winners. From L to R: Jim McMahon, Earl Campbell, Peyton Manning, me, Don McPherson, and Gino Torretta. *(Photo courtesy of Florida Sports Information)*

grudge marathon matches where we battled for hours playing racquetball.

Coach Stephens was one of those old-school coaches who didn't just teach football, he molded character. He delivered 20- or 30-minute "sermonettes" before every practice, preaching to us what it took to become a champion. He would spell out the word "CHAMPION" on the blackboard and use each letter to teach us a little about competition and life. "C" was for Character, "H" stood for Heart, "A" was for Attitude, "M" for Mental toughness, "P" for Poise and Pride, "I" was Initiative, "O" was for Others, and "N" was for Nerve. It is funny how something like that can stick with you into your adult life.

When Coach Stephens came into team meetings and started talking, he demanded your full attention. If you didn't look him in the eye, there was trouble. He'd constantly gaze around the room, and if he didn't see your eyes—boy, oh boy, that was bad news. During one of his prepractice speeches, one of our players not only wasn't looking at Coach Stephens, but actually fell asleep during the meeting. Poor soul. Can you imagine waking up to a thunderous voice and a mountain of a man shaking you by your collar, banging you up against the wall and spraying tobacco juice all over while he's yelling at you?

We respected and feared Coach Stephens. He was firm, but fair. One of the best athletes in our entire school—a guy who could win the shot put, the discus and the 100 meters at a track meet—was kicked off the team by Coach Stephens because of his bad attitude. Coach Stephens wanted his players to be dedicated and committed to the team. And it paid off. My senior year, we went 14-0, winning the state championship and sending 13 players off on college scholarships.

As I've grown, I've enjoyed a new relationship with Coach Stephens as a friend. We've shared many experiences together over the years and have become quite close. All of us who played for him at Fort Walton Beach High School owe Jimmy Ray Stephens so much. He not only helped develop us as players, he helped develop us as young men.

PEYTON MANNING

In my opinion, Peyton Manning will without question go down as one of the greatest quarterbacks in college and professional football history. The best thing about that is this: Despite all he has accomplished, he never beat me in head-to-head competition. I say that both proudly and humbly…and excitedly. In all the years at Florida, and one overtime win in the National Football League, I was always fortunate to be on the winning team. I think that's quite an accomplishment because Peyton is such an incredible student of the game.

Obviously, Peyton comes from a great football family. His father, Archie, carries himself with tremendous class in New Orleans, the city where I now live. And it's no secret that NFL scouts also believe his brother Eli—the top player selected in the 2004 draft—is a great talent. Peyton and I often cross paths at banquets and other events, and we enjoy a casual friendship. He's been very generous to charities in New Orleans and Indianapolis, and his foundation has even helped us begin our athletic program at Desire Street Ministries, the inner-city ministry I work with in New Orleans.

The media always made a huge deal about the rivalry between Peyton and me. In my opinion, there was more hype to it than substance. The fact of the matter is there are rarely rivalries between quarterbacks. I looked at it like I was playing against Tennessee's defense and Peyton was playing against our defense.

Peyton and I played in some big and memorable games. I just feel very fortunate that I ended up on the right side of the win column in every one of them.

CHRIS DOERING

Chris is one of my favorite people. We have had a great relationship ever since we met in college. Through our initiation into big-time college football at Kentucky in 1993 (for all the non-Gator readers, that was the game where I threw Chris a 28-yard touchdown to win the game as time expired), all the way through Chris's final game in the 1995 Fiesta Bowl, we just seemed to have a certain chemistry. One of the most disappointing things about my college career is that Chris left a year ahead of me and didn't get to be a part of the magical 1996 season. As special as that season was, it would have been even more special if Chris had been there to share it with us.

Our relationship continued beyond college, and one of the highlights of my NFL career was when Chris and I both got a chance to play together again with the Washington Redskins. We reconnected and spent time with his wife, Tiffany, and their daughter, Taylor. They now have a new son, Tyson. The Doerings have been great friends, and Chris was an unbelievable teammate.

You know someone is special when you smile and laugh every time they cross your mind. That's what happens when I think of Chris. He's a goofball, but he's a tremendous friend.

JAMES BATES

And speaking of goofballs, James Bates is one of the most colorful personalities I've ever known. He's incredibly talented in all that he does, and I think he's found a great niche for himself now as an actor and commentator. The guy's been crazy ever since I met him at UF, when he was throwing water balloons at fraternity guys. James would do so many off-the-wall things. He used to get into the shower and sing "O Canada!" at the top of his lungs. He showed up once at Halloween with a football helmet carved out of a pumpkin. He can do impersonations incredibly well, and I remember at different times on the team bus, he'd get on the loudspeaker and crack up everybody with different impressions of people. It was amazing. He would have all of the voices and nuances down perfectly. At one time or another, everybody on the team attempted to do an impersonation of Coach Spurrier, but James had him down the best.

James could take any situation and transform it into quite a dramatic experience. One summer, he came to visit my family in Destin when my brother Ben, who was 11 years old at the time, was playing with a neighbor. The friend was a girl who seemed to always be pestering and badgering poor Ben. Well, this particular day she claimed she could do 150 push-ups, and Ben challenged her.

"You cannot do 150 push-ups," Ben said.

"Can too," she said.

"If you can do 150 push-ups," Ben said, "I'll give you my Nintendo."

Well, James Bates was in the house, and he turned this little debate into a major pay-per-view sporting event by doing the play-by-play broadcasting of this little girl's attempt to do 150 push-ups. She got down on the floor, and the challenge began. With James calling the shots on a make-believe microphone, there was plenty of drama when she hit 75. My brother started sweating when she got to 100. We were all in disbelief when she reached 140. The drama then reached an incredible and hilarious crescendo as she slowly conquered each of the last ten. I will never forget the moment; she did all 150 push-ups! My brother had to weasel his way out of his bet, and we witnessed one of the greatest commentaries of all time.

Early in our UF careers, reporters would often mistake James and me because we looked so similar. Reporters would approach James thinking he was me and start asking him questions about the quarterbacks. And James, being the clown he was, would sometimes play along. Once, a reporter wrote an entire story about me, but all the quotes were from James, who was posing as me. It just so happens those were the most glib and colorful Danny Wuerffel quotes in the history of journalism.

And I guess that's the one thing I'll always remember about James Bates: He was one of those guys who made football incredibly fun.

JASON ODOM

I've already shared many stories about Jason throughout this book, but he's meant so much to me—on and off the field—that I feel he should be mentioned here, too. Jason was my roommate all through college and remains one of my best friends on the planet. We had sort of a brotherly relationship when we lived together, and obviously we're still brothers in our faith in the Lord. I've enjoyed staying in touch with Jason and his family, and it's been great to watch him grow as a man and a Christian.

LAWRENCE WRIGHT

Lawrence Wright is the Gator who took a simple phrase to another level: "If you ain't a Gator, you're Gator bait!"

What an amazing guy—an incredibly talented football player and pillar on our defensive squad during the SEC Championship run. Who could ever forget the devastating blow Lawrence put on a poor Tennessee receiver in 1995? He threw caution to the wind and catapulted his body into the unsuspecting wide receiver, disrupting both the receiver's attempt to catch the pass as well as his normal brain activity. I can still hear the collision; I'll bet the receiver can still feel it.

Off the field, he was just as full of color and charisma as he was on it. He always had something dynamic to say, but Lawrence wasn't just talk. He worked as hard as anybody to become a great athlete and a good student. He majored in building construction and persevered even though it was a very difficult task. He overcame many odds, coming out of the Liberty City section of Miami. And I've always been so impressed with his willingness to give back to his community.

Even when he was in college, Lawrence had already developed a program to help underprivileged kids in his hometown.

Last time I talked to Lawrence he had just gotten married, started four or five businesses and was pursuing life just like he used to pursue ball carriers—at full speed. In the NFL, a team once cut Lawrence and on his way out he told them, "The next time you see me, I'm going to own this team. In fact I'd like to thank you for cutting me, because why would I want to be a millionaire when I can be a billionaire?"

DONNIE YOUNG

Donnie was a bull in a lot of ways; one tough hombre. He was an incredibly determined football player and an absolute rock on the offensive line. I can't tell you how many times the guy would limp out on the field and play with an injury. He could have a dislocated shoulder or a sprained knee, and it didn't matter. I could always count on Donnie Young to do his job and protect my back.

You want to know how tough Donnie was? He suffered a severe ankle injury in the third quarter against Florida State in 1994—the year the Seminoles rallied from 28 points down in the fourth quarter to tie us 31-31. After the game, Donnie was hobbling off the field on crutches when he heard a fan swearing at his father. Donnie had to be restrained by athletic director Jeremy Foley because he was trying to get into stands to let the fan have it with one of his crutches.

Donnie didn't talk a lot, but when he did, the team respected what he had to say. When we were playing Florida State for the national championship in the 1997 Sugar Bowl, there's a story about one of our offensive linemen staying out late partying in the French Quarter. Donnie went up to him after practice one day and said, "If you're going to be out on

The hog-hunting crew takes a trip to Venice, Florida. The group includes Jeff Mitchell, Donnie Young, Anthony Ingrassia, and Jason Odom along with Donnie Young's friends and family. I am in the center of the bottom row.

Bourbon Street acting like that, I'm packing my bags and going home, because you're not going to be ready to play." This particular teammate wasn't seen on Bourbon Street again until after the game, when we were celebrating the national championship.

Donnie was from Venice, Florida. And while it's true that Venice Beach is a hot spot for northern snowbirds and retirees, it's also home to some of Florida's best hog hunting. Yes, hog hunting. In fact, Donnie used to gather up several of us Gators to spend a weekend in Venice on the hunt for dangerous attack hogs. At first, I thought it was a joke. The only hog I could picture was cute little Porky Pig, and I didn't want to shoot little Porky. But apparently there are several types of hogs, and the Venice hogs snorted, growled, had long tusks as sharp as razor blades, and were very scary.

One might ask how we fared in our hog-hunting escapade. Well, the first successful thing was that the hogs didn't eat us. The second? We had some great pork BBQ compliments of Danny Wuerffel's eagle eye and sharp shooting. I still claim I was the best marksman in the group and bagged the most beasts. I'm sure Donnie and the rest of the crew might disagree, but this is my book.

SHANE MATTHEWS

My first year at the University of Florida, Shane Matthews was the quarterback, giving me the opportunity to watch and learn from one of the greatest signal-callers in Southeastern Conference history. I can't tell you how instrumental that experience was to my own development as a quarterback. Shane is one of the most laid-back people you could ever meet, and he used that to his advantage as a player. Shane would just let things roll right off his back. As he would put it, "I'm just a good ol' dude." But don't let him fool you. Actually, he's a very intelligent football player who's been in the NFL for a decade now. You don't stay in the league that long without having some ability and some savvy. He has really created quite a niche for himself.

After UF, Shane and I played together with the Chicago Bears and the Washington Redskins. We've been through many highs and lows together. From the day he hosted me during my recruiting visit, I have valued his friendship and his guidance.

TERRY JACKSON

Terry Jackson is a very rare and special athlete. He was one of the few guys who I really believed could have played any position on the football field. And he nearly did. I'm just thankful he didn't play quarterback or I might not be writing this book.

During his career at Florida, Terry played offense, defense, and special teams, and he played them all well. He could adapt to any position or situation. After he went to the NFL, there were some who believed Terry wouldn't make a very good pro. The logic was that since the NFL is so much more specialized and streamlined than college football, Terry's versatility wouldn't be as valuable a commodity. Well, once Terry got to the NFL with the 49ers, he went on to have a productive career, and we're all proud of him for what he's accomplished.

IKE HILLIARD

Ike is truly one of the greatest receivers to ever play at the University of Florida. He, too, was an amazing athlete who was a spectacular runner after he caught the ball. Remember the catch he made against Florida State in the national championship game? I still don't know how he was able to catch the ball, come down, stop on a dime, back up while the two defenders ran into each other, and then gracefully trot into the end zone. My anterior cruciate ligament would still be lying on the field at the Superdome if I had tried it. That catch defied all the laws of physics, but Ike defied a lot of odds.

Even when we both got to the NFL, Ike and I stayed in touch. One Christmas, at the end of a particularly tough season with the New Orleans Saints, I got one phone call from someone other than my family: It was Ike Hilliard, just calling to say "Merry Christmas." I'm just so thankful to have played with him and to still be his friend.

REIDEL ANTHONY

While Ike was an extremely physical receiver with powerful legs, Reidel was probably the most graceful receiver I played with at Florida. He reminded me a little bit of Jerry Rice because he was so smooth and fluid. He really turned it on during our senior season when he made big play after big play when Ike wasn't able to play for a couple of games. Reidel had blazing speed, a smooth stride, and a relaxed attitude. Whether he was running a fade route with grace and precision or returning a kickoff for a TD, Reidel always found a way to make a difference in a game.

JACQUEZ GREEN

Can you imagine being the quarterback of a team with Ike Hilliard and Reidel Anthony as your starting receivers, and the No. 3 guy coming off the bench was Jacquez Green? I was lucky to be able to play with so much talent. Jacquez was a couple of years younger than I was, but despite his age, he was incredibly productive for us during the 1996 season.

His speed was amazing and deceptive. The guy never looked like he was running full bore. In fact, it almost looked like he was jogging, but he was actually moving faster than anybody on the field. That's why I think he was able to get open. He would lull defensive backs into a false sense of security and then—boom!—the next thing they knew he was running right by them.

Jacquez also had a great mind for offensive football. I wouldn't be surprised if he ended up as an offensive coordinator one day.

FRED TAYLOR

Fred Taylor was an amazing athlete, a pure blend of speed, agility and power. He came in really highly recruited and was a couple years behind me, but it was great to watch him mature as a football player. Fred was just a natural who had all the tools—speed, size and the natural instincts that all of the truly great runners possess. When he was healthy, Fred was one of best running backs in college football. And now he's one of the best running backs in professional football.

ERIC KRESSER

The first I heard of Eric Kresser, he was the prototype high school quarterback with a cannon for an arm. There was no question about it, he was an incredibly talented player who could have had a phenomenal career at Florida. I guess it just wasn't in the cards for Eric to be the quarterback at Florida, so he ended up making a smart decision and transferring to Marshall after the 1995 season. At the time, Marshall was I-AA, which meant Eric didn't have to sit out a year before he could compete. As it turned out, he led Marshall to the I-AA national championship the same year we won the national title in the Sugar Bowl. During his years at UF, Eric helped me be a better quarterback, and I'm just thrilled he got the chance to win a national title, too.

ERRICT RHETT

I say this in a nice way, but Errict was a mess. When I think of him, a big smile comes across my face. Errict was a guy who always wanted the ball. "Give me the ball," he used to say endlessly. "Give me the rock and let me go to work." After most passing plays, he'd come back to the huddle and say, "Man, I was wide open. Wide open! You should have thrown me the rock." Later, the tape revealed he actually had three or four guys covering him like a blanket.

One time, he saw Brett Favre hand the ball off to a running back and then do some crazy jump-pass fake. It looked more like a Kareem Abdul-Jabbar skyhook than a football move and I'm certain it didn't accomplish a thing. But Errict thought it did, and he would make the QBs try the same move. It was easier to comply and look like a fool than to listen to Errict go on and on about it.

BRIAN SCHOTTENHEIMER

Brian Schottenheimer transferred to UF from Kansas, but it wasn't so much to play as it was to learn from Coach Spurrier. He came to Florida as a backup quarterback, but his intent even in college was to become a coach like his father Marty Schottenheimer, who has been an NFL head coach for several years. Brian's plan was to transfer in and play for the Gators while studying and soaking up Coach Spurrier's knowledge.

Even as a player, Brian had a coaching air about him. He would talk in coach-speak and knew more about the Xs and Os of football back then than I'll probably ever know. I also owe Brian a debt a gratitude for teaching me how to dress. When Chris Doering left, Brian became my roommate on the road. Until I met him, I didn't realize that you could fold dress pants by the seam and hang them upside down so they stay really nice and smooth. I just always kind of threw them on a hanger and let them get all wrinkly. So anytime you see me now in nice-looking pants, all the credit goes to Brian Schottenheimer.

JEFF MITCHELL

Jeff Mitchell was a good friend from day one. He started off as a defensive player at Florida, and I thanked the Lord often in my prayers that they moved him to offense. He became the anchor of our line and one of the best centers in the country. Jeff was a great player and an even greater friend.

SHAYNE EDGE

Shayne Edge had the mentality of a linebacker and the physical skills of the position he played: punter. He always added drama, no matter what the situation was.

He was a great punter for us and made some incredible plays—both punting and running the ball on fake punts.

BART EDMISTON

Bart is a friend of mine dating back to high school, when I quarterbacked at Ft. Walton Beach and he kicked at Pensacola Washington. Our team beat his team our last two years of high school, and he never really got over that. In fact, he still insists the referees cheated Washington when we played them during our junior year.

In all honesty, Bart remains one of the most skilled kickers I've ever seen. I used to watch him time after time make 10, 15, 20 field goals in a row. He worked tirelessly and was a phenomenal talent, and I was really disappointed that he didn't get to experience all the success that I did. He had some adversity and some bad things happen at the wrong time, so that was unfortunate. But all turned out well. Bart is finishing up medical school right now, and he and his wife, Beth, are great friends of ours.

NOAH BRINDISE

When I knew Noah in college, he was just a typical good ol' college boy and a real goofball. Every third word that came out of his mouth was just hilarious. You never knew exactly what he was talking about or where he was coming from. He was a walk-on reserve quarterback during my senior season at Florida. The next time I ran into Noah, he was my quarterback coach with the Washington Redskins. It was unbelievable to see how much he had developed and what a great coach he had become. Now he is the offensive coordinator at East Carolina, and I think Noah Brindise has a bright future in the coaching business.

RON ZOOK

People often ask me if I ever played for the Gators when Ron Zook was on the coaching staff. Actually, four of the five years I played at UF, Coach Zook was there as either the defensive coordinator or special teams coordinator. The thing that stood out about Coach Zook is that he always had more energy and adrenaline than any coach I've ever seen. Now that he's a head coach, his tenacity and work ethic have become legendary, but he was the same way as an assistant.

I'm excited that he is now our head coach at the University of Florida, and I believe he has what it takes to be successful. During the 2003 season, when the Gators were going through some tough times, Coach Zook asked me if I'd be willing to come over to Baton Rouge (from my home in New Orleans) to

speak to the team before it played against LSU. Believe it or
not, the team was staying at the same hotel in Gonzalez,
Louisiana, that we stayed in when we won the national title in
the Sugar Bowl in 1996. I got a chance to speak to the team
during chapel service, and later that day, the Gators went out
and beat the Tigers 19-7.

I'm sure there are a lot more things that went into it, but
one of the things I can now take credit for is praying for the
Gators before we beat the national-champion LSU Tigers.

BOB STOOPS

I think Bob Stoops is one of the greatest coaches in college
football. His defensive expertise, along with his player-friendly
style of coaching, provided us the extra spark we needed to win
the 1996 national championship. The aggressive style of defense
he brought from Kansas State added the final weapon to
Spurrier's Gator arsenal. With a high-powered offense and a
dominating defense, we were virtually unstoppable in 1996.

I'm still a big fan of Bob Stoops, and many of my
Louisiana neighbors couldn't believe I was cheering for the
Sooners in the 2004 Sugar Bowl when they played LSU for the
national title. And even though I think Coach Stoops will go on
to be one of the most successful coaches in college football
history, he may not even be the most successful member of his
own family.

His wife, Carol, had so much success selling Mary Kay
beauty products that she received a pink Cadillac—Mary Kay's
highest award. I guess the pink Caddie is a little like the Coach
of the Year award and the Heisman Trophy all in one. I wonder
if Coach Stoops, even after a couple of national titles, doesn't
feel like he'll always be living in her shadow. It's been rumored
that you might even catch a glimpse of him taking a late-night

spin in a pink convertible Cadillac through the rolling plains of Oklahoma. I doubt it.

JERRI SPURRIER

Coach Spurrier's wife, Jerri, is a special person that I'll never forget. She has a genuine concern for others and is one of the kindest, most warmhearted women I've ever known. When one of the Gator players had a birthday, she would always bake the player some cookies. And, let me tell you, it was always a treat to get a batch of Mrs. Spurrier's chocolate-chip cookies.

One thing I will never forget is what incredible shape she was in. One year, she ran 10 miles from their house to the stadium to watch a game. That just blew me away. She also used to teach an aerobics class and a couple of times she invited the players to take part in her class. We thought our strength and conditioning staff was tough until we got in there with Jerri Spurrier. She really wore us down.

BOBBY BOWDEN

Some Florida fans might not like to hear it, but I have a lot of respect for Bobby Bowden. He spends much of his time in the community, speaking at various events, youth groups and churches. He's also very active in the Fellowship of Christian Athletes, which is an organization near and dear to my heart.

The longevity of Bobby Bowden's career is simply amazing. How can you not have some admiration for the program he has built? There is no question that if you listed the premier programs in the second half of the 20th century, Bobby Bowden's Florida State Seminoles would be right near the top. And if you'd told anyone that would be the case three decades

My brother Ben leads this mountain bike adventure around Rampart Reservoir in the Colorado Rockies.

ago when he took over an abysmal program in Tallahassee, they would have laughed at you.

You know, FSU used to be an all-girls school. At least that's one thing us Gators will always be able to laugh about.

JON WUERFFEL

I don't think I could possibly have a chapter in my book about personalities and not include a section about my father.

My father is a really unique and amazing man, and growing up with Jon Wuerffel as a dad made for quite an entertaining childhood. He is a retired Air Force Chaplain and spent his life as a pastor, but he's far from your stereotypical man of the cloth. He's an avid motorcyclist who once rode cross country with the Hell's Angels; he scuba dives with a big spear gun; he parachutes out of airplanes; he rides through the

My dad and I take a break during a motorcycle trip along Florida's
Gulf Coast.

mountains on bikes—motocross and bicycles; he's won national
tournaments as a racquetball player and spots me 10 points in a
game to 15 just to make it competitive. He's 60 years old now,
and he can still wear me out.

My dad says he used all the different activities to help me
develop a sense of toughness and coordination. He says I
wouldn't have become much of an athlete without all the
different sports and hobbies we did together. That's what he says
now, but I suspect he just wanted somebody to play with back
then.

He absolutely loved being active—and he never knew
when to quit. If we didn't get lost at least two or three times on
a motorcycle adventure through the mountains of Colorado, it
wasn't a successful trip for my dad. I still remember the time one
of my dad's buddies in Destin owned a parachute, and my dad
got this idea that he was going to make his own parasailing rig.
So he hooked the parachute to the back of our boat, but he

After a motorcycle ride in the Rockies, my dad and I enjoy the view along the front range.

didn't quite get it right and ended up dragging my little brother 100 yards through the water. Of course, he claimed he was just toughening him up, too. Those signs you see on the professional parasail boats—"Don't Try This At Home"—they just presented a new challenge for my dad.

One time when I was in the fifth grade, we went on a motorcycle ride through the Rocky Mountains. The only problem was the snow hadn't completely melted off the mountain. No big deal for my dad who was on this 500 cc KTM—a big bike with lots of clearance. However, I was on a little Kawasaki 80 with no clearance. Once we started going through the snow, I had to keep putting my feet down because the bike kept slipping out from under me. I was wearing big, heavy motorcycle boots and after about 45 minutes of constantly putting them down and lifting them back up again, my legs became completely fatigued. I couldn't even lift them back up on the foot pegs and I ended up dragging my feet through the snow for the rest of the ride. I was completely exhausted and absolutely miserable, but my dad was determined to make it all the way up the mountain. Man, was I mad at him that day. I spent many years of my childhood just hoping to get back home safely to Mom.

Another time, my dad and I were motorcycling along a mountain road when I hit some rocks and got twisted sideways. As I was falling backwards, I accidentally pulled back on the throttle, accelerated and was about to launch off the side of the mountain. Somehow, my front tire hit square on the side of the tree, compressed the shocks, bounced me back onto the road and I kept going as if nothing had happened. Even back then, I knew God was looking out for me.

Oh, the stories I could tell. Like the Christmas morning we went scuba diving and my dad dumped me and my brother-in-law, Ray, into the freezing water off the coast of Destin. The visibility was about three feet, and I quickly lost sight of Ray in the murky water. You're never supposed to lose sight of your dive buddy, so I sat at the bottom of the anchor rope and waited, hoping Ray might somehow find me. Finally, my air ran out and I felt like I was going into hypothermia so I swam back to the surface as mad as I could be. Somehow, Ray had made it back alive as well, and we both could think of several better options to celebrate Christmas morning. But, according to my dad, we came up a lot tougher than when we went down. He thought of it as a complimentary Christmas toughness training seminar. At least we didn't run into any sharks. Well, at least not on that day, but that's another story.

I kid my dad because I love him. There aren't enough words in this book to explain how much my parents have meant to me. I grew up in an incredibly positive and Christian home, and I'm still learning of the ways my parents have helped shape my life. When the New Orleans Saints drafted me in 1997, they made every rookie take a psychological evaluation. The psychologist told me: "Based on this exam, it's obvious to me that you grew up in one of the most positive and supportive environments that there could possibly be." I'm more and more aware of it, and I can't possibly express my gratitude to my parents for their sacrificial and unconditional love.

CONCLUSION

I could probably continue this chapter forever. While trophies and rings are great mementos from special seasons, they can't possibly compare to the amazing people that have cemented a place in my heart. And while there are many more that deserve to be mentioned, I'll have to save them for another book.

7

ALMOST BUT NOT YET: MY JUNIOR SEASON

I was a giddy Gator going into my junior season. I felt like we had a great squad, we were loaded with talent and I was really starting to get a firm grasp of Coach Spurrier's offense. Of course, we would know soon enough just how good we were because the highly ranked Tennessee Volunteers were coming to the Swamp for the third game of the season. That game was one of the greatest experiences of my life and actually set the tone for the incredible and exciting offensive fireworks that would be our trademark for the next two years.

EVEN COACH SPURRIER WAS IMPRESSED

Tennessee jumped ahead of us 30-14 late in the first half, but what followed was one of the most unbelievable displays of offense that I've ever been a part of. We came back to score the next 48 points (this is not a typo) and won the game 62-37. We scored touchdowns on seven straight possessions against one of the best teams in the country. Even a torrential downpour in the second half couldn't stop us from scoring more points against the Volunteers than they had given up since a 70-0 loss to Duke in 1893. And Coach Spurrier wasn't even at Duke then, although Norm Carlson might have been. (Norm Carlson was the sports information director at UF all the way back to when Coach Spurrier was in college.)

I threw for six touchdowns that day, which tied an SEC record for most TD passes against a conference opponent. Everything was working to perfection. Our receivers were running free all day long, especially Ike Hilliard, who tied a school record with four touchdown catches. It just seemed like we could almost call our shots that day.

In fact, at the end of the game, when we were way ahead, all we were trying to do was run out the clock. That's when I turned to running back Terry Jackson in the huddle and said, "OK, I want you to run 80 yards on this play, but don't score a touchdown. And make sure you stay in bounds so the clock will keep running. Got it?"

Terry didn't exactly follow instructions. He only went 66 yards.

"Sorry," Terry told me afterwards with a big smile on his face, "but at least I stayed in bounds."

Even Coach Spurrier, who was always pushing and prodding us to be better, seemed astounded by what we were able to do that day. "It was one of the best offensive games that I ever coached or ever watched," he said.

When I look back on my junior and senior seasons, this was the game where we really established ourselves as an offense—sort of like the launching of a rocket ship, where everything just sort of exploded and we took off. When our offense was working, it was amazing to be a part of it. This game was like that. It was like going through your plays in practice, when you're completing every pass and scoring on every play.

PEYTON'S PLACE—NOT ON *SI*

This was also the game where the media began making a huge deal out of the so-called rivalry between Peyton Manning and me. Peyton was the up-and-coming star of college football, and *Sports Illustrated* had spent a week in Knoxville preparing to do a big cover story on Peyton after our game. But because the game went south for the Vols and we put up so many points, I ended up being on the cover of *SI* that week instead. Talk about being a blessing—and a curse. Do you know how many thousands of people in the country collect every *Sports Illustrated* and try to get the person on the cover to autograph it? To this day, I still get that *SI* cover in the mail with a request for me to sign it.

At the end of the Tennessee game, there was this incredible rain that just capped off a wonderful day. There is a picture someone took of me at the end of the game where the raindrops are flaring off my uniform and my hands are clasped in prayer as I lead my teammates off the field. If you're interested in seeing the picture, check out the cover of this book.

BATTLE BETWEEN THE BUSHES (I MEAN HEDGES)

Later that year, we went and played Georgia in Athens. They were renovating the stadium in Jacksonville, so for two

I'm rolling right and looking downfield for a receiver.
(Photo courtesy of Florida Sports Information)

years we played at the home stadiums—my sophomore year in Gainesville and my junior year in Athens.

I didn't grow up entrenched in the traditions of the Southeastern Conference, so the significance of the Gators playing "Between the Hedges" in Athens for the first time since 1932 was sort of lost on me. It certainly wasn't lost on Coach Spurrier. While the players all loved to play against Florida State and considered the Seminoles our biggest rival, that wasn't the case with Coach Spurrier. He played in an era of Gator football when Georgia was the most important game, and that mind-set continued even when he was coaching. The Georgia games were extra special to him. He took great pride when we played well against the Bulldogs, and he really got a kick out of beating them the way we did during the 1990s.

During my years at the University of Florida, we beat the 'Dogs every way and everywhere. We beat them in Jacksonville, we beat them in Gainesville, and this was our chance to beat them in their own backyard. "This is probably the only time in our lifetime that we will play up here," Coach Spurrier said before the game. "Let's go out there and make it a memorable game for all Gators."

Did we ever! We won the game 52-17, I had one of my most efficient statistical games ever and we broke our own record (set against Tennessee) for touchdown passes in a Southeastern Conference game. I completed 14 of 17 passes for 242 yards and five touchdowns, and Eric Kresser came in and threw two more touchdowns. Our offense was once again making it look easy. So easy, in fact, that Chris Doering actually pulled down three touchdown passes—in the same possession. But only the last one counted because the other two were nullified by penalties. The game was very memorable for me, but more on that later.

RUNNING UP THE SCORE

Some of the Georgia fans and media were unhappy with Coach Spurrier because Eric threw the final touchdown pass (on a flea-flicker) with 1:10 left in the game to backup wide receiver Travis McGriff. Some might say that was running up the score, but Coach Spurrier always had the philosophy that the backups deserve a chance to pitch and catch, too. The reason you put backups in the game is so they can get some experience running our offense, and our offense was based on throwing the football. I always liked Coach Spurrier's analogy about Nebraska. He would always say, "Why is it that when Nebraska gets way ahead, nobody criticizes them for continuing to run the ball?" Good point. When running teams are way ahead, nobody expects them to all of the sudden start throwing the ball. But when throwing teams get way ahead, the backups are expected to come in and start running the ball.

Coach Spurrier was also big on making history. That last touchdown gave us 52 points, and as he would say afterward, "We knew coming in that no one had ever scored 50 in this ballpark. It was something we wanted to do. You always like to do something nobody else has ever done."

After the game, a few of our players broke off little pieces of Georgia's famed "hedges" as mementoes. Said Dexter Daniels, one of our linebackers, "This hedge is going to be my little piece of history. I'm going to take it home and put in a book."

In hindsight, Dexter's quote seems pretty appropriate. For all Gators, that victory over the Bulldogs was definitely one for the books.

DESERT MEMORIES

We were undefeated during the regular season and played against the Nebraska Cornhuskers in the Fiesta Bowl for the national championship. A lot of people don't know this, but when I was in fourth grade in 1983, we lived in Lincoln, Nebraska. Mike Rozier, Nebraska's talented tailback, won the Heisman Trophy that year. Turner Gill was the quarterback and Irving Friar was the star receiver. If you'll remember, the Cornhuskers were undefeated in 1983 and were being billed as

I'm getting ready to throw a pass at the Swamp.
(Photo courtesy of Florida Sports Information)

perhaps the greatest college team in history. They played in the Orange Bowl against the Miami Hurricanes, who had a young quarterback named Bernie Kosar. I'll never forget how the Huskers scored a touchdown at the end of that game and were down by a point with hardly any time left on the clock. Instead of kicking for a tie and probably a share of the national championship, Coach Tom Osborne went for two. When the two-point attempt failed, I was crushed and so was the rest of the state of Nebraska. You would have thought that a war had been lost in Lincoln that night.

Like I said, I was a big-time Nebraska fan as a kid and continued to follow the Cornhuskers throughout the years. I watched them play and loved them—all the way until that desert night we played them in the Fiesta Bowl. My feelings about Nebraska haven't been the same since.

MOTORCYCLE MEMORIES

Right before the Fiesta Bowl, we got a break for Christmas vacation and had a few days to go visit our families. At the time, my parents were living in California, so I flew out for a quick visit before reporting to Tempe for the bowl game.

Growing up, one of our favorite hobbies—it's still one of my dad's favorite hobbies—was to ride off-road motorcycles. One of my most vivid memories as a child was riding motorcycles all through the Rocky Mountains in Colorado with my dad. We spent a lot of quality time together barrelling through those mountains.

Well, my dad was stationed at Edwards Air Force Base in California (the place where the Space Shuttle often lands in the desert) before the Fiesta Bowl. The California desert made for some great motocross riding. My dad always got excited whenever I came home, because it gave us a chance to do the things we used to do together—like riding motorcycles. He always enjoyed the father-son riding time and the excursions through the woods and trails. Well, I've got to tell you: It's really not a great time to go riding motorcycles right before the Fiesta Bowl. I was a little worried about doing anything remotely dangerous before such a big game, but my dad kept imploring,

"Oh, come on, you can go. We'll put all the best safety equipment on you and just make sure you drive slowly and are very careful." I finally agreed and put on all the gear, and off we vroomed through the desert. But I've got to tell you, I was probably the slowest-riding motorcycle dude on the planet that day. I'm not sure if anybody—and certainly not Coach Spurrier—ever knew I was out riding motorcycles just a few days before the biggest game any of us had ever played in.

THE FIASCO BOWL—DISASTER IN THE DESERT

We went into the Fiesta Bowl and, for whatever reason, Nebraska just absolutely demoralized us. They beat us every way you can be beaten. They were a strong, tough, and fierce team that came into the game driven and determined. The disappointing thing for us is that once we got behind, we didn't have the deep character as a team to turn it around. For the first time, I really felt like some of our guys gave up a little bit. It's one thing to get beat—even badly, but it's another thing to get frustrated and shut it down. I was always taught that through rain or shine, good times or bad times, you always play until the final whistle blows. If you don't, bad turns into worse and things can snowball out of control. Well, we were in the desert, but there was plenty of snowballing. When the game finally ended, we had been embarrassed 62-24. It was the most lopsided loss in a No. 1 vs. No. 2 matchup in college football history. That's not a distinction to be proud of.

We played sloppy and undisciplined. We had eight penalties for 68 yards in the first half alone. We had a hard time blocking them (I was sacked seven times and we gained minus-28 yards rushing) and tackling them (they gained an incredible 524 yards on the ground). I made several poor decisions and bad

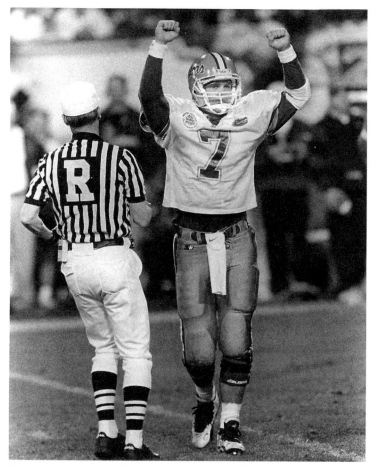

I'm enjoying a short-lived celebration at the Fiesta Bowl against Nebraska. *(Photo courtesy of Florida Sports Information)*

throws. I don't know how many times after the game we saw that highlight of Nebraska quarterback Tommie Frazier breaking loose on a 75-yard run, where it looked like he broke about 47 tackles and eluded about 35 of our defenders. I think the only Gator who didn't miss a tackle on that play was Mr. TwoBits.

It was a very frustrating time for all of us, and Coach Spurrier made the comment afterward that if we had played them 10 times, he thinks they would have beaten us all 10 times. I don't think that was necessarily true. I still believe that in different circumstances and another time, we could have done a lot better.

If there was any solace in this game, it was that we were beaten by maybe one of the great teams of the modern era. That was Nebraska's second consecutive national title and it could have been its third consecutive if not for a missed field goal against Florida State in the 1993 Orange Bowl.

I think it served as a great learning experience for us. As a team, we may have been too relaxed going in and we were riding the fence between confident and overconfident. We were taught a great lesson that night. We learned you just can't show up. We learned that a good, old-fashioned, hard-working team can give a nice, newfangled flashy team a butt-whipping anytime and anywhere.

YOU GOT WHAT I NEED

However, I should have had a premonition that the Fiesta Bowl was destined to be a disaster. ABC ran a little video clip of Chris Doering and me in the intro prior to the game, and I think it foreshadowed the debacle that would follow.

Chris majored in telecommunications production at UF, and one of his projects was to produce a television segment featuring a musician. Chris's job was to coordinate the whole show, directing the cameramen, audio specialists, and lighting technician—he was even the executive editor for the whole deal. He had a pretty big job. The insignificant part of the whole thing was the musician. It didn't matter who it was, or even how talented they were. In fact, he didn't even want to bother his good musician friends with such a small gig. Just any old guy would do. So Chris called me. I could play the piano a little bit, and he tricked me into thinking this would be my big debut.

I showed up at the studio and things seemed to go just fine. I played a few old hymns, some classical music and even the first good song I ever learned to play on the piano, the love theme from *St. Elmo's Fire*. Chris did a stellar job of orchestrating the event, his assistants were extremely efficient, I didn't make many blunders and the whole event took less than 30 minutes. And all would have just been dandy if we had just shut the deal down and walked out then.

But as they were turning off the lights and putting away the equipment, Chris sat next to me and we started goofing off. I started playing Biz Marqee's 1990s hit rap song, "You Got What I Need." It's a cool rap with a catchy piano part, but the chorus of the song is what will haunt me forever. In the middle of his cool rap, Biz attempts to sing this chorus:

"You, you got what I need, but you say he's just a friend, you say he's just a friend.

"Oh baby, you, you got what I need, but you say he's just a friend."

It really sounds a whole lot more like he's screaming it than singing it, and he's really not the finest vocalist you'll ever hear.

But if you want to be a good impressionist—if you really want to make people laugh—you have to imitate the original as best you can. And we did. We sang and sang away. I rapped each verse and then we'd join together screaming the chorus at the top of our lungs. We had a blast and everybody was rolling ... including the tape. Who'd have thought his teacher—whom we thought was in the production booth to shut things down—couldn't pass up the opportunity fire up the camera and catch the whole show on tape.

But that's not such a bad thing, is it? One woman in Gainesville with a video of a couple of college guys acting and sounding like idiots isn't such a big deal. Not until she sends it to national network and they air it on national television just before one of the most watched TV events of the year. We were humiliated in more ways than one that night in the desert, but what can you do?

HEADLINE: SPURRIER LEAVING FOR THE NFL

A few days after that Fiesta Bowl meltdown, we were hit with some more distressing news: There were rampant rumors that Coach Spurrier was thinking about leaving for the NFL. Every year, it seemed, some team in professional football pursued Coach Spurrier and, for the most part, we tried not to pay much attention to it. But this time there was real concern. I knew something was up when Coach Spurrier called Eric Kresser and me in for a meeting. He told us he was seriously considering leaving for the Tampa Bay Bucs. I thought it was very professional and thoughtful for him to tell us even though he was still mulling over it. But it was still a disturbing bit of news.

As the evening progressed, the news kept spreading and reporters kept calling. I called Coach Spurrier and talked with him; I hoped he would stay, but I wanted to let him know I'd support him in whatever he did. It was an anxious time for fans, players and everybody associated with the University of Florida.

Our athletic director, Jeremy Foley, became so concerned he left the NCAA convention in Dallas at 5 a.m. the next morning, thinking he might have to start looking for a new football coach. When he arrived back in Gainesville, Jeremy was asked by reporters what his night was like knowing Coach Spurrier might leave. He replied: "I slept like a baby—I woke up every five minutes crying."

When I went to bed that night, I still didn't know what Coach Spurrier's decision would be. But the next morning, the *Gainesville Sun* reported that the decision was made: Coach Spurrier was leaving. There was a huge headline and even a list of Coach Spurrier's most likely successors. Later that morning, though, I learned, "You can't believe everything you read in the newspapers." That was always one of Coach's favorite quotes.

Coach Spurrier told us he decided to stay at UF. We were all thrilled and extremely relieved. He held a news conference and told the media: "Coaching the Gators is what excites me the most. After thinking about it, I just believe this job is the best for me and my family. My roots are awfully deep here. Maybe I'm just a college ball coach."

Looking back now, I'm ever so thankful that he didn't go to the NFL that year. As we all know, the following season turned out to be something very special for Coach Spurrier, for me and for the entire Gator Nation.

8

THE HEAD BALL COACH

WHAT MADE SPURRIER GREAT?

I get asked all the time: Why was Steve Spurrier such a great college football coach? I think it's because he was a paradox, an enigma, because he had a combination of two qualities that seem to be so contradictory.

First of all, Coach Spurrier was very much a detail-oriented coach, almost hyper detail oriented in terms of the route running by the receivers, the precision of the patterns, the drops and head-positioning of the quarterbacks and the timing of the play. Coach Spurrier wanted everything run perfectly and always wanted his quarterback to be able to call the right play at the line of scrimmage to best take advantage of the defensive alignment. So in one sense, he was extremely detailed.

But on the other hand, he had this backyard, draw-it-up-in-the-dirt mentality. He had this carefree, fly-by-the-seat-of-your-pants approach like, "We can do that. We can do anything we darn well please." A writer once wrote that Coach Spurrier relied on "the precision of a mechanical engineer and the imagination of a sandlot player in devising his offense." That's pretty accurate.

Usually, you get a coach who's one way or the other. There are some guys who aren't really detailed; they are the ones who are too aggressive and too risky, but don't have the scheme to back it up. But more often than not, you get coaches who are at the other end of the spectrum, who are so bogged down in details that they're afraid to try anything out of their realm. Mostly, these are the safe, conservative coaches who like to run the ball, control the clock and play defense. Coach Spurrier had the unique ability to combine the two qualities to become one of the greatest college coaches in history.

STUPID PET TRICKS

The only thing you could be sure of with Coach Spurrier is that you couldn't be sure of anything. And it was this unpredictability that made him so great. I always appreciated that Coach Spurrier never fit the mold. Sometimes, he was ultra-serious; other times he was incredibly light and comical. If a coach is a taskmaster every second of every day, it can be really draining on the players. Coach Spurrier, on the other hand, was often lighthearted and funny.

I remember once we were watching a game tape of the Georgia Bulldogs, and Coach Spurrier kept showing one play over and over again. He rewound the tape again and again, and none of us players knew why. Finally, Coach Spurrier said, "Ya'll don't see it, do you?"

Of course, we didn't know what he was talking about.

"Ya'll don't see it?" Coach asked again.

See what?

I'm getting some last-minute coaching points from the Old Ball Coach.
(Photo courtesy of Florida Sports Information)

I'm posing for a Heisman photo with Coach Spurrier. He was the first person to win the Heisman Trophy as a player and then coach a player who won it. *(Photo courtesy of Florida Sports Information)*

"The dog," he said, pointing out Uga, the Bulldogs' ugly, saggy mascot. "Look at the dog!"

Sure enough, the dog was jumping up, twisting in the air and landing on its back in a hilarious manner. We all burst out laughing. And that's what I mean about Coach Spurrier not fitting the mold. Football can be a grind, and a lot of coaches make it that way. Coach Spurrier always tried to mix in some fun.

LEARNING THE ROPES

In any relationship the ability to communicate is critical. And the really special connections occur when you get to know someone so well that you often know what they are thinking or feeling without them having to verbalize it.

I think one of the reasons I had such success with Coach Spurrier was because I was able to internalize his offensive philosophy and react accordingly during the course of a game. But after working that closely with someone for that many years, you also tend to learn a lot more about them than just how they would dissect a zone defense or run a double-reverse pass.

For instance, Coach Spurrier loved to ask questions. He'd constantly ask football questions to see if the players were paying attention and learning their assignments. He'd also ask weird football trivia questions just for fun—like who was his head coach at Florida or who knew the high school Errict Rhett went to and so forth. Since I was one of the recipients of his barrage of questions for so many years, I began to notice a trend: If he thought you knew the answer, he'd skip you and ask someone else. This became very valuable and clandestine information, and I'm sharing it now for the first time.

You see, I learned to always nod my head like I knew what he was looking for, and if he ever asked me if I knew the answer, my response was always, "yes" whether I had a clue or not. Once he bought the "yes," he moved on and asked some other poor victim, "What position did Charlie LaPradd play for the 1952 Gators?" This little trick saved me countless times and helped distinguish me as the quarterback who always knew what Coach Spurrier was thinking.

THE FUN 'N' GUN

Whether I knew all of his thoughts or not, I did understand the offense. It was based on creating mismatches, and I think there are a number of reasons why we were so successful in accomplishing that. It starts with the fact that we had great athletes, and don't let anybody tell you that you can be a dominant team without having great athletes. No system works unless you have the players to make it work. And, believe me, we had the players to make it work. When you have receivers like Reidel Anthony, Ike Hilliard, Chris Doering and Jacquez Green, you ought to be able to pass the ball.

Secondly, Coach Spurrier's philosophy was so unique. I remember hearing him say one time: "There are two ways you can be successful. You can do what everybody else does and try and work harder and do it better. Or you can do something totally different." Coach Spurrier wanted to do something totally different.

He had a scheme and a grid that was just so very different from what most people were used to. It was hard for opposing defensive coordinators to game plan against us and figure out what defenses to run. And Coach Spurrier just had this uncanny knack of being able to look at a defense and figure out immediately what would work against it and where it was most vulnerable. If he spotted a weakness in one area, he went after it like a pitbull. He'd keep running the same play the whole game if the defense didn't make adjustments. We'd play a whole game with no huddle or no running backs; some games we'd use two tight ends and one running back if that's where the defense was most susceptible.   Coach Spurrier almost had a defensive mentality on offense. He wanted our offense to be the aggressor and he wanted defenses to fear us.

FADING AWAY

One of my favorite Coach Spurrier routes that we ran was the fade pattern. Earlier in my career at Florida, we would face a whole lot of zone coverage and we were putting up some pretty big numbers against it. Then during my junior season, LSU played bump man-to-man coverage and gave us some trouble.

(The same thing happened in a devastating Fiesta Bowl loss to Nebraska that season.)

Going into my senior year, one of things we wanted to do was run more quick slants and fades. The fade was so effective because the receiver takes off like he's running a quick "go" route, but the quarterback takes a three-step drop and lets the ball go almost immediately. The idea is to fade the ball over the receiver's shoulder near the sideline when the defensive back doesn't know it's coming. We worked and worked on the pattern and it became something we did really well. It was a play we had such great confidence in even when the receiver was covered like a blanket. I can only imagine how frustrating the play must have been for opposing defensive backs because if it's run right against the right defense, it's virtually unstoppable.

COACH'S SIDELINE "VOCABULARY"

People often wonder how I dealt with Coach Spurrier's intense sideline demeanor and "colorful" vocabulary. Believe it or not, through my experiences in the NFL, I've actually come to realize how amazingly clean Coach Spurrier's vocabulary is on the sidelines compared to many other coaches.

I'll never forget one year, my freshman year, when Coach Spurrier was on the sidelines letting off some steam when things weren't quite clicking on offense. The next day at practice, he said, "Danny, come over here with me. We're going to go to the other sideline and practice signals."

It seemed a little bizarre to go all the way across the field just to practice the signals, but I followed him over to a remote corner of the practice field. Once we were there, we ran a play or two and he said, "Danny, when you were in high school, did

Coach Stephens (my high school coach) ever get frustrated and maybe say a bad word or two?"

I replied, "Maybe just one or two."

Coach Spurrier looked at me and said, "Yeah, I try not to and I usually don't, but every now and then one slips out."

And then he clapped his hands and said, "OK, my man, let's go on back over to practice."

I think that was just Coach Spurrier's roundabout way of apologizing. And to a young quarterback, the gesture meant more than he could have ever known.

The fact is, a football stadium with 100,000 fans screaming at you is an intense environment and people say a lot of things that they wouldn't say in a normal situation. And Coach Spurrier, as we all would come to learn, was a very intense competitor.

In life, certain people tend to bottle things up; other people wear their feelings on their shirtsleeves. I tend to not express things much; my wife rarely holds back—and if anything is bothering her, you're going to hear about it. Coach Spurrier was a little more like that. He always told you what he was thinking, no matter what. A lot of people get frustrated and can't get over it. But Coach Spurrier could get frustrated with me over something that happened during a game and—in a moment—turn around and call another brilliant play.

My response to Coach Spurrier's emotional sideline demeanor was to very much pay attention because he was being critical of things that happened on the field. I would heed his words, try to learn from them, but also be aware that no one can see everything during the course of the game.

Yeah, there were times when I became frustrated on the sideline, but I never considered talking back to him or getting visibly angry. It would be counterproductive. There'd be no purpose in it.

Besides, I always felt Coach Spurrier was simply playing the game vicariously through us. He was so intensely into the game, it wouldn't have shocked any of us if he'd grabbed one of our helmets, ran onto the field and played a series or two himself. Believe me, I'd much rather play for a coach who pushes you to perfection rather than one who accepts mediocrity.

TURKEY DAY WITH THE SPURRIERS

In my opinion, there are several ways to get close to people and one of those ways is just by experiencing things together. When you go through ups and downs together, you feel a connection with people, and Coach Spurrier and I have certainly been through a lot together over the years. From the day I met him when I was being recruited to our trying times together with the Washington Redskins, we've been through tremendous highs and tremendous lows. I definitely feel there's a connection and a special relationship that we will always have.

Every Thanksgiving he would have the quarterbacks over to his house for dinner, and we'd always watch the NFL games on TV. Those were fun and special times. In fact, I still vividly remember one of those times at his house during my sophomore year. We were getting ready to play Florida State, and our quarterback situation was a little unsettled. Terry Dean had played part of the year at quarterback and I had become the starter later in the year.

That week, Derrick Brooks, Florida State's great linebacker, had made a statement in the media that he expected to see Terry Dean sometime during the game. Coach Spurrier came up to me on Thanksgiving and said, "Danny, did you hear where Derrick Brooks said he thought Terry Dean was going to play?" And then he said, "I want you to go up to him as soon as the game starts and tell him, 'I'm going to be in this game the whole day so you better get used to seeing me.'" As sophomore, it's pretty special to hear your coach say something like that. When you're young and timid, you sometimes need strong words of encouragement and that was Coach Spurrier's way of encouraging me.

THE QUARTERBACK SHUFFLE

As everybody knows, the quarterback's job is never safe with Coach Spurrier. When I was a freshman, the constant change didn't really bother me, because I didn't have any expectations and I felt playing half the time was better than none at all. I was simply grateful for any playing time I got. But by the time I got to my sophomore year, it became more difficult to handle. That was the year he went with Terry Dean the whole first half of the year and then everything switched and I played the second half of the season.

I think there are two sides of the coin when you're talking about quarterback stability. One of Coach Spurrier's favorite quotes is from legendary former UCLA basketball coach John Wooden, who once said, "The bench is a coach's greatest ally." I think that's absolutely true when you're dealing with one of five players on a basketball court, but sometimes I wonder if it's as relevant in the context of a quarterback on a football team. But the bottom line is Coach Spurrier has had success—and a great amount of success—doing it his way.

I have to tell you, though, I believe it would have been very hard for me to function in the system that Coach Spurrier implemented after I graduated. That's when, for a time, he was switching quarterbacks every play. I believe there is more to playing quarterback than what happens on the field. I don't know if there's any position in all of sports like being a quarterback. As a starting quarterback, you have to develop relationships—camaraderie and chemistry with your teammates—and I think those bonds are integral to the success of a team. However, at the same time, if I were coaching and I had two guys who could really play, it would be very difficult for me to keep one on the sidelines if the other was struggling.

Some people may question Coach Spurrier's methods, but they can't question the results. There is no question in my mind that he pushed me to be better than I could have been in other situations. You never know what might have happened had I gone to Florida State or Alabama; you just never know. I'm just thankful I had a chance to play for and learn from Steve Spurrier.

I feel blessed to have played for him and I hope he feels blessed to have coached me. We've got great memories that will last a lifetime.

One thing he told me when I graduated was, "Danny, even if you go off and play pro ball, you'll never, ever experience the joy you did in college football."

Truer words were never spoken.

Looking back over my career and having been blessed to play several years in the NFL, I can assure you of one thing:

Nothing compares to the memories we made and the championships we won at the University of Florida with Steve Spurrier as the Head Ball Coach.

9

GATOR GLORY: MY SENIOR SEASON

HIGH SCHOOL REUNION

Not many people remember our game with Division I-AA Georgia Southern during my senior season, but it was particularly rewarding for me. One of my best friends from high school, Eric Thigpen, was the starting free safety for the Eagles. It was the second game of the year, and we were coming off a lackluster performance against Southwestern Louisiana. It was important for me to have a good game and for our offense to play well against Georgia Southern. As much as I tried not to pick on my old high school buddy, I completed 15 of 16 that day and had one of the most efficient games of my career.

Eric grew up an avid Gator fan while I, as mentioned earlier, gravitated toward Florida State. It was actually in Eric's ninth-grade yearbook that I drew a picture of a Seminole stabbing a Gator. Well, after I completed 15 of 16 against Georgia Southern, Eric came up to me after the game, reminded

me of the yearbook drawing and said with a chuckle: "Looks
like you've become a Gator through and through now."

BLOWING THE TOP OFF
ROCKY TOP

I'd be remiss to look back on my college career and not
draw special attention to the Tennessee game we played in
Knoxville my senior year. Once again, it was built up as a Game
of the Century, but, then again, we played a lot of Games of the
Century that year. I've often wondered what the legal limit is on
Games of the Century because we might have surpassed it and
could still be susceptible to NCAA sanctions.

This was another Danny Wuerffel vs. Peyton Manning
dynamic duel in Knoxville, where the stadium had just been
expanded and the largest crowd (107,608) in college football
history was crammed into the place. Not only that, but
supposedly the largest media contingent in Southeastern
Conference history was jammed into the press box at Neyland
Stadium. Reporters from *USA Today*, *Sports Illustrated*, the *New
York Times*, *Los Angeles Times*, *Chicago Tribune*, *Washington Post*,
Atlanta Journal-Constitution, *Boston Globe*, *Houston Chronicle*,
Dallas Morning News, *Philadelphia Inquirer*—well, you get the
idea—were there to record this historical moment in modern
world civilization. This game was so big that one of the radio
stations in Knoxville trumpeted the fact that it had performed
"the world's longest pregame show,"—a show, they said, which
began eight months earlier in January. That's how crazy the
people are in the Southeastern Conference about their college
football.

Truly, it was an amazing experience and atmosphere in
Knoxville that day. My faith in God really affected my attitude
going into the game and gave me a sense of peace that freed me

After we played Georgia Southern my senior year, I got a quick picture with my old high school teammate and great friend, Eric Thigpen.

up to play without any doubts or hesitation (see more on this in the "Faith and Football" chapter).

Although we were on the road playing in the most hostile environment imaginable, we were unfazed. In fact, it was almost like our offense picked up where it left off the year before, when we scored 41 unanswered points against Tennessee in the second half. This time, we didn't wait until the second half. We jumped out to 35-0 lead—with 10 minutes still remaining in the first half. That bears repeating: There were 10 MINUTES STILL REMAINING IN THE FIRST HALF!

Astonishing. We were on pace to score 100 points against the No. 2-ranked team in the country. I've had a lot of great feelings in my college career, but this ranked right up there: What a tremendous pleasure it was to hear 107,000 screaming fans become dead silent in a matter of minutes. Said our comedic linebacker James Bates, who went to high school in Tennessee: "It got so quiet, I thought the Tennessee fans had left early to check out *The Jeff Foxworthy Show*." This was one of the most surreal experiences of my life. It was pouring down rain that day in Knoxville, and in the first half, it seemed like touchdowns were raining from the sky, too.

FOURTH-DOWN FRENZY

Believe it or not, one play on our opening series probably made the difference in the game and set the tone for our season. We faced a fourth and 11 from Tennessee's 35-yard line and, sure enough, Coach Spurrier decided to go for it. It turned into one of the most climactic moments of that whole season, because there is no telling the different directions that game could have gone based on that one play. One thing I learned to expect from Coach Spurrier is that you could never know what to expect. That's what I believe separated him from most everybody else: His willingness to try things other coaches wouldn't.

"We were shocked when they decided to go for it," Tennessee cornerback Steve Johnson said at the time.

Most coaches would have either tried a long field goal or a short punt, but Coach Spurrier, as we all know, is not most coaches. Going for it on fourth down was commonplace for him. His philosophy was to score as many touchdowns as possible, and if you have four chances to do it, why only take three? We went for it on fourth down five times that day in Knoxville, and we made it all five times.

"I wonder sometimes if he forgets he has a punter," our punter Robby Stevenson said after the game. "But the guy has guts. He usually makes it. What am I going to do? Complain when we're scoring?"

Our defensive end Tim Beauchamp probably summed it up best: "If Coach Spurrier went for it on fourth down inside of our own 5-yard line, I wouldn't be shocked at all."

But Tennessee was. I'm not sure the Vols knew what was coming. Most likely, they were thinking we would be looking to get a first down with some sort of mid-range, 15-yard corner route. They guessed wrong. Coach Spurrier wanted the whole enchilada and called a post pattern to Reidel Anthony. A reporter asked me afterward if I had audibled to the play at the line of scrimmage and my response was something like, "Yeah, right, like I'm going to have the nerve to call a post route on fourth and long."

That was Coach Spurrier's call, and as I dropped back to pass, I could see out of the corner of my eye that the safety didn't get deep. I launched the ball to Reidel, who was open and caught the ball in stride in the end zone for a touchdown. Neyland Stadium went from an insane asylum to a morgue. One second it was deafening; the next second you all you could hear was the soft sound of the rain hitting the field.

"Such a nice quiet," was how our running back Eli Williams explained it. "You could hear yourself think. And what I was thinking was, 'Man, this feels good.'"

That one play totally changed the atmosphere and helped pave the way for one of the most amazing seasons in Florida football history. After the 35-29 victory, our fans held up signs that said, "Citrus Bowl needs Volunteers," and "This ain't Peyton Place; it's the Wuerffel House." And as we trotted off the field, they serenaded us with, "It's great ... to be ... a Florida Gator!"

Those words certainly rang true then.

And they ring true now, too.

ROLLING THROUGH THE SEC

The first half of the Tennessee game was a precursor to how good our offense would become. We would really find out a few weeks later during a dominating three-game stretch against LSU, Auburn, and Georgia.

We beat Tennessee on the same day Arizona State shocked No. 1-ranked Nebraska, which made us No. 1 in the country. Historically, the Gators have not handled the No. 1 ranking very well, but this time was different. We were a team filled with veteran players, and we knew that the hype surrounding No. 1 was just that—hype. We were determined to stay focused and continue getting better. We weren't going to allow ourselves to get overconfident, and Coach Spurrier certainly wouldn't allow us to get the big head.

We beat LSU 56-13, Auburn 51-10 and Georgia 47-7, and outgained those three traditionally tough SEC opponents by an incredible 1,788 yards to 748. The offensive records were piling up every week. We beat LSU by the largest margin ever at Florida Field and ran up an SEC-record 635 yards of total offense. The 51 points against Auburn was the highest in series history and the 625 yards of offense was the most Auburn had given up in 100 years of playing college football. The 40-point victory over the Georgia was most the Gators had ever won by in the series.

Even Coach Spurrier was astounded. Usually, he wasn't a coach who heaped on the praise, so we must have been playing incredibly well for him to be gushing like he was.

After we beat LSU, Coach Spurrier said, "This might be the best game we've ever played here."

A week later, after we beat Auburn, he said: "This might be the best game we've ever played, maybe even a little better than last week."

Then a game later, after we beat Georgia, he said, "I keep thinking, 'It can't keep going this well,' and dadgummit it, it just keeps happening. Hopefully, it will keep happening the rest of the way, but it just amazes me how they keep coming out and playing well. Danny Wuerffel has been sensational, the receivers, the running backs, the offensive line and the defense. I'm just really proud of the entire team."

I don't know which one of those games was the most satisfying, but I do know this: Coach Spurrier really wanted to beat LSU that year. The year before, LSU "held us" to 28 points and even though we ended up beating them 28-10, LSU defensive coordinator Carl Reese was supposedly putting on coaching clinics on how to stop the Fun 'N' Gun.

Two days before we played LSU in 1996, Reese actually drew up some of his schemes in a halftime feature on ESPN's Thursday night game. After we put up 56 points on LSU, Coach Spurrier was quoted as saying, "Hopefully, their defensive coordinator won't be giving any clinics next year on how to stop the Gators."

Even when I think back on it now, I still wonder if those three games really happened. Everything we did during that span seemed to work. Our offense was explosive, our defense was shutting down opponents and getting turnovers; we were a complete team in every way. It was like we were running plays in practice, where everything works perfectly. It was that stretch of games that put us in position to win the national title.

LATE HITS AND SNITS

By the time the end of the season rolled around, it was time for yet another Game of the Century, this time against the mighty Seminoles at Doak Campbell Stadium in Tallahassee. Both teams were undefeated, and the winner would be the odds-on favorite to win the national championship. It had been eight years since a No. 1 and No. 2 had met so late in the regular season and 23 years since they had faced each other in the final regular-season game when both teams were undefeated.

We obviously didn't know it at the time, but that FSU game would start the ball rolling on one of the most amazing, unlikely and incredible months of our lives. From highs to lows, to lows to highs, what a whirlwind of emotions and sensations it turned out to be.

When people ask me what my most memorable game was, I tend to think of all the games where I threw a bunch of touchdowns or we clinched some sort of championship. But for a lot of people, they tell me the most memorable game I ever played was when Florida State beat us 24-21 in the last regular-season game of my senior season. Even though we lost the game and statistically I didn't play well, I guess fans were impressed because I actually walked off the field under my own power.

My dad told me later that he counted, and I got knocked down 32 times in that one football game. What I've been told by several people is the courage I displayed in getting back up is what they remember the most. Even several Heisman Trophy voters told me later that this was the game that they decided I had earned their vote.

Even though our offense broke almost every school record that year, it seemed like our offensive line was always in a state of flux. Believe it or not, we had eight different starting offensive line combinations during that championship season, and our line was banged up and patched together by the end of the season. Center Jeff Mitchell, our rock in the middle and the core of the offensive line, was injured a couple of weeks before the Florida State game, which wasn't a good omen considering the Seminoles had arguably the best aggregation of defensive line talent that college football had seen in years. Their defensive front four was incredible with guys like Peter Boulware, Reinard Wilson, and Andre Wadsworth—all of whom would go on to become first-round draft picks in the NFL. They were tenacious pass rushers and played an extremely physical style of defense. Coach Spurrier obviously thought they played too physical, as he would argue several times leading up to the rematch in the Sugar Bowl.

I always let Coach Spurrier and others talk about whether Florida State played dirty in that game. I never thought it was my place to second-guess the officials or the other team. That just wasn't my personality, and once Coach Spurrier even told the media, "Sometimes, I wish Danny would get a little madder at those guys who are hitting him late."

Yes, Florida State played aggressive, and football is an aggressive sport. The problem is that college football doesn't protect the quarterback like they do in the NFL. I think college football allows too much leeway in letting the quarterback get hit. Certainly, a lot of those hits Florida State administered would not have been acceptable in the NFL. The officials called a couple of late hits against them and there were certainly a few more they could have called. But it just made it all that much sweeter the next time we played them.

CRANBERRY CRUNCHED

I was told once that the way they find out if a cranberry is a healthy fruit and if it's the right density is to test it for resiliency; to see if it actually bounces. The way they test cranberries is to roll them all down an incline, drop them off a little ledge, and if the cranberrry bounces a certain height, it's a good fruit that can be sold at the market. If it's too soft and doesn't quite bounce high enough, it's thrown away. So, in a sense, the good fruits are the ones that bounce back.

I've never forgotten that story, and I've sort of adopted it as a philosophy for my life: When things are going bad and you get knocked down, you bounce back up and don't make a big deal about it. I certainly got a chance to put that philosophy to practice against Florida State.

I was sacked six times that day and got smacked nearly every time I threw the ball. I was told later that I was taking such a beating that my little brother Ben was crying in the stands. Afterward, one of our team trainers said I looked like I'd been in a gang fight. I had cuts and bruises and welts all over my body. I hurt so much that I couldn't even hug my mom after the game.

Todd Fordham, one of Florida State's offensive lineman, said at the time: "They called some of those Miami-Florida State games the Game of the Century. This is the Game of the Last Two Centuries."

Little did we know at the time, we would be playing the Seminoles again just a few weeks later in The Game of the Millennium.

A TEAM OF DESTINY

As the weeks progressed following the loss to Florida State, an unbelievable set of circumstances transpired that allowed us to get back into the national championship picture. When everything goes right in life, you experience a certain level of enjoyment. But when you go through some adversity and overcome it and then end up on top, there is a more profound sense of heartfelt appreciation. I think we certainly appreciate our national championship even more because of the roundabout route we had to take to win it.

We were the No. 1 team in the nation before we lost to Florida State—and never had anybody lost a game so late in the season and had any realistic chance whatsoever of winning the national championship. For all intents and purposes, our national title hopes were dashed once again after the Seminoles beat us.

I remember some very difficult practice days after the game and a lot of frustrated players and coaches. But one of the things I think was different about our team from the previous year (when Nebraska routed us in the Fiesta Bowl) was that we had matured. The character and the senior leadership really started to kick in as we got ready for the SEC Championship Game the following week against Alabama.

I remember James Bates, Lawrence Wright, and several other seniors being adamant about not allowing an attitude of frustration and surrender to infiltrate the team's psyche. We would not allow ourselves to think all was lost that day in Tallahassee. I think that was a tremendous testimony to the character of our team. We got ready, we prepared ourselves to go win a conference championship, and we kept telling ourselves that we could be the first senior class in history to win four consecutive SEC titles.

HOOK 'EM HORNS

We were in our hotel in Atlanta the day of the SEC Championship Game, and Coach Spurrier and I were riding the elevator up to the team floor. Like I mentioned earlier, Coach Spurrier was one of those coaches who liked everything to be quiet and serious when we were preparing to go play in a big game. Well, when the elevator door opened up, the entire floor was yelling and screaming and erupting in chaotic cheers. Coach Spurrier didn't know what was going on. At first, I think he was angry because he thought the team was goofing around when we had such an important game coming up in a few hours. We were quickly informed that Texas quarterback James Brown had just completed a gutsy fourth-down pass in his own territory to lead the five-loss Longhorns to a shocking upset of No. 1-ranked Nebraska in the Big 12 title game.

In other words, our biggest play of the day took place before we even stepped on the field against Alabama. It was the Cornhuskers who were supposed to play Florida State in the Sugar Bowl for the national title, but now we had a chance for a rematch if we just took care of our business against the Crimson Tide. As Coach Spurrier said, "God gave us a mulligan." And we certainly put it to good use. We were so pumped up about Texas beating Nebraska that we went out and had a phenomenal game against Alabama and ended up winning 45-30. I threw six touchdown passes, and the 45 points were the most ever scored in an SEC Championship Game and the most Alabama had given up in 26 years.

What an unbelievable run our senior class had in the SEC. The win over Alabama gave us four consecutive conference titles and was our 22nd consecutive conference victory. As we left the field, our fans chanted, "S-E-C! S-E-C! S-E-C!" Those three letters reverberate through my mind even today.

DAD PULLS SHOTGUN ON COACH SPURRIER

After the SEC Championship Game, there was a flurry of awards shows and ceremonies all over the country to attend. It was during a trip to Louisville, Kentucky, for the Johnny Unitas Golden Arm Award, where my dad's chat with Coach Spurrier may have altered the history of Florida football. OK, maybe it wasn't that dramatic, but we'll let my dad think it was.

My dad ran into Coach Spurrier in the men's room at the banquet hall where I was about to receive the Johnny Unitas Award. It was right there in the bathroom (I hope they weren't side by side at the urinal) where my dad finally got a chance to share his thoughts on offensive strategy with Coach Spurrier. My dad always thought we should run more of our offense from the shotgun formation because he thought it would give me more time and allow me to see the field better. Coach Spurrier actually agreed with him that day and designed our whole offensive game plan in the rematch against Florida State around the shotgun. I'm sure Coach Spurrier had already figured it out—and, in fact, we had used quite a bit of shotgun in the SEC Championship Game—but my dad likes to take credit for it.

COMING UP ROSES

The Sugar Bowl had sort of become our second home during my career at Florida, and we were familiar with the lay of the land. This was my third Sugar Bowl as a player and Coach Spurrier's fourth as a coach. From past experiences, Coach figured out that staying in the French Quarter could become quite a distraction for the players, so after a few days practicing in the Big Easy, he checked us out of the Hilton Riverside hotel and we headed west. We got on a bus and left the madness of New Orleans behind and travelled to the small, quiet town of Gonzalez, Louisiana, about 45 miles away. We should have known something very good was in store for us when we walked into the hotel lobby and saw they had an actual live gator frolicking in the fountain out front. OK, so it was small baby gator and it was really chained and in the arms of a zookeeper, but it was still cool. We checked into our rooms in Gonzalez just in time to watch the end of the Rose Bowl—the final piece of the jigsaw puzzle that had to fall into place before we could play for the national title.

There was still an undefeated team—Arizona State—ahead of us in the polls, and if the Sun Devils beat Ohio State in the Rose Bowl, there was no way we could win the national title even if we beat Florida State. You better believe we were all huge Buckeyes that night. Our hearts sunk into our guts when Arizona State quarterback Jake Plummer made an incredible run and somehow found a way to reach the end zone with just over a minute left to give Arizona State a 17-14 lead. But somehow Ohio State rallied and marched 65 yards to score the winning touchdown with just a few seconds left.

I guess you could say our national championship celebration started a day early because everybody was running around the hotel room courtyard, hugging and high-fiving and celebrating Ohio State's victory. I'm sure Florida State probably heard us yelling all the way back in New Orleans. It was hard to maintain our composure that night. There was just incredible excitement and anticipation; the same sort of feeling we experienced a few weeks earlier when we celebrated in our Atlanta hotel after Texas upset Nebraska. Everything, it seemed, was falling into place for us, and we began getting this euphoric feeling that a national championship was meant to be.

I'm not much on autographed memorabilia, but months after we won the national title, I received an autographed football in the mail. It was from Ohio State's football coach, and all it said was: "To Danny: You're Welcome. John Cooper."

I remember after we won the national title, Coach Spurrier said we should include John Cooper and Texas coach John Mackovic as people who deserve a championship ring. I don't know if they ever got their rings or not, but, at the very least, we certainly owe them a huge debt of gratitude.

LATE HITS REVISITED

People often ask me how the "late-hit" controversy affected me before the Sugar Bowl, and I can honestly say it had no effect on me whatsoever. I let Coach Spurrier do all the talking and I just prepared myself for the game.

As we all know now, Coach became so angry after watching the game film of the regular-season finale against Florida State game that he compiled a tape of the uncalled late hits and sent it to the SEC office. "When you watch the replays, these guys aren't just shoving Danny down," Coach Spurrier said, "They're loading up, they're hitting him under the jaw with their helmets, they're spearing him, they're burying him."

Coach Bowden, as you might expect, tried to diffuse the situation with his homespun humor. "We maybe stop hitting at the echo of the whistle instead of at the whistle itself," he cracked.

There were those who believed Coach Spurrier was practicing psychological warfare; others believed he was just plain mad. Whatever the case, he was adamant and defiant. In one news conference before the Sugar Bowl, he even said, "Maybe we're declaring war on the Seminoles. We're going to try to play like they do. We're not going to try to hurt their quarterback, but we're not going to take the same crap we took up there in Tallahassee. I told the players that, and they like that idea."

I remember once somebody asked Coach Spurrier why he was so upset about the situation, yet I was so calm and never became involved in the controversy. Coach Spurrier's reply was something like, "Because I'm an Old Testament guy and Danny's a New Testament guy." It was a cute and funny way of Coach saying that his philosophy was "An eye for an eye," and my philosophy was, "Turn the other cheek."

Coach Spurrier put all the pressure squarely on his own shoulders and even told the media the day before the game, "If we lose, you can go ahead and blame me. That's OK." He had created a massive turbulence around himself heading into the game, which allowed me to remain amazingly relaxed in the eye of the storm. Even though we were playing a Florida State team that had won an NCAA-record 11 consecutive bowl games, I felt as calm and confident as I ever had heading into a game.

THE FUN 'N' SHOTGUN

Maybe the reason I felt so assured before the game was because we were going to run most of our offense in the shotgun, which we felt would counteract Florida State's fierce pass rush. And the beauty about Coach Spurrier was this: He wasn't content just to put in the shotgun, he added in some of the strangest twists and freakiest formations you can imagine. But our formations weren't the only strange things that happened that night in the Super Dome.

Early in the game, Coach Spurrier and I were on the sideline discussing some game strategy and one of our band members actually tapped me on the shoulder and asked me for an autograph. This was DURING THE GAME! Oh my goodness, you should have seen the look Coach Spurrier gave that poor girl. I mean, you would have thought Ray Goff had just barged his way into our sideline conversation. It was a look of total and complete disdain.

There was another memorable experience on the sideline that night involving my dad. The TV network had brought him down on the field to interview him during the game, so he had a media credential to stand on the sideline. I guess because he was on the sideline, this gave him the idea that he was an assistant coach. As I mentioned before, just after the SEC Championship Game, my dad had urged Coach Spurrier to use the shotgun. Since my dad considered the shotgun to be his idea, he thought he had a right to coach me up on it during the Sugar Bowl. He came behind me on the sideline in between offensive series and said, "Danny, you're not doing it right. You've got one hand up and one hand down when you're catching the snap from center; you need to have both hands up." This was directly opposite to what Coach Spurrier had told me. I can just remember looking at my dad incredulously and thinking, "What in the heck are you doing here?"

At any rate, we used the shotgun almost exclusively and it worked to near-perfection. Usually, Coach Spurrier had one of our backup quarterbacks flashing in the signals for the plays, but not for a game of this magnitude. There was too much riding on it. He signalled in plays directly and did everything but run out on the field and shout out the plays himself in the huddle. The shotgun allowed me to have an extra microsecond more time to throw, which enabled me to get the ball off to Ike (Hilliard) and Reidel (Anthony). I ended up throwing for 306 yards and three touchdowns, and we won the game 52-20—the most points the Seminoles had given up in more than a decade.

Our offensive line played incredible that night, and Bobby Bowden said they must have taken to heart Coach Spurrier's controversial comments about late hits.

"Those remarks evidently had a great effect on his ballclub," Coach Bowden said. "They were made to us, but the way his offensive line responded they were listening. They said to themselves, 'It's not going to happen again.' If we were going to beat Florida again, we had to get to Danny Wuerffel, and we just couldn't."

MEDIA BLITZ

You want to talk about a bittersweet moment. As soon as the game ended, I was as exhilarated as I've ever been. I was so filled with joy and excitement, I could hardly contain myself. All I wanted to do was get with my teammates and celebrate. The problem was there were more members of the media on the field than there were fans in the stadium, and they all wanted a quick, personal interview with Danny Wuerffel. It must have been a comical sight watching me trying to elude all the newspaper reporters and TV cameramen in almost the same way I had tried to elude Florida State's pass rush just a few minutes earlier. The media was chasing me all over the field, and I was scrambling like Michael Vick. I've always tried to be accommodating with the media, but this was one time when I was in no mood to be interviewed. I just wanted to find a teammate to hug.

BOURBON STREET BEDLAM

I didn't make it out to Bourbon Street that night with a bunch of our other players, but I heard it was a madhouse. Five months earlier, Coach Spurrier proved to be prophetic when he gave a speech to the Jacksonville Gator Club and predicted that Gator fans would be "hugging and high-fiving on Bourbon Street in the wee hours of January 3." And that's exactly what they were doing after the monumental victory over the Seminoles. I heard Coach Spurrier tried to make an appearance on Bourbon Street about 3 a.m., but could only make it a few steps before he was enveloped by the celebrating masses. He quickly retreated back to the team hotel.

There's another story about Terry Jackson walking into a McDonald's in the French Quarter a few hours after the game. But there was a long line filled with fans, so Terry turned to walk out. Suddenly, all those giddy Gators recognized Terry and started applauding. The people sitting down in the booths gave him a standing ovation. And, before he knew it, the line parted like the Red Sea and Terry was standing in front of the register ordering his food.

A reporter from the *Miami Herald* asked Reidel Anthony if I was going to make an appearance amid the debauchery on Bourbon Street that night and he just shook his head, smiled and said: "Man, if Danny stepped foot in here, God would start making it rain so hard that everyone would leave."

I guess what Reidel meant was that Bourbon Street isn't exactly my cup of beer, er, tea. I actually celebrated with my family at the house of Dave Kruger—one of my dad's classmates at the seminary who lived in New Orleans. I've always thought that celebrations are more about who you're with than what you're doing. Good times mean being with good people, and, let me tell you, we had a great time that night.

When Coach Spurrier accepted the national championship trophy the next morning, he said: "God has smiled on the Gators. We were a team of destiny."

As I reflect back on it now, I'm so thankful things worked out like they did. With all the unlikely set of circumstances that came together at the end of season, it really made our championship seem more magical and special. We didn't control our own destiny until that very last game, and then we went out and did our part. We played a fantastic game, and it was the climax to a wonderful year.

A dream game ending in a dream season, which was the perfect and fitting ending to a dream career.

CELEBRATE GOOD TIMES, COME ON!

What if there was no game and 60,000 people still showed up?

That's exactly what happened at the national championship celebration that was held for us at Florida Field a few days after we beat Florida State. They told us about 30,000 people would probably show up, but, incredibly, nine days after the championship, twice that many people were still excited enough to pile into the Swamp for a day of jubilation. They came from all over the state, and they were young and old and rich and poor. Because it was a free event, it was neat to see a little bit different crowd at Florida Field that day. As great as it is to attend games at the Swamp, as the years go by, it gets more and more expensive, and not everybody can afford it. That's why it was great to see the faces of some of the kids who normally weren't at the games.

I can remember Jeff Mitchell standing up and telling the crowd, "We've got more fans at this thing than Florida State gets for a home game." It truly was amazing how many people attended. And as I looked out over the fans that day, it was another reminder of how unbelievably loyal and passionate Gator fans are.

Sometimes, I think we forget how much college football means to the fans. The players come and play for the institution and we become Gators at that point, but many of these fans have been Gators for 30, 40 and 50 years. Many of them waited a lifetime for us to win a championship, and then there are so many more who never got to see it.

The celebration was probably more special to me than a game because, for the first time, I really got a chance to enjoy the fans, hear their cheers, and read their signs. You don't really pay attention to the crowd when you're playing because you're

One of the perks of being famous—I got the chance to fly in a fighter jet. Although, I didn't buzz the tower, I did feel like Maverick from the movie *Top Gun*.

I'm teeing off on a par three at Augusta National. I played the course and the course won.

so focused on the game, but I got a chance that day to see just how blessed we Gators are to have such tremendous fan support.

We walked into the stadium on a cool, sunny Saturday and made a big circle around the field, slapping hands and hugging all the fans who were sitting in the front row. Just looking at the joy in the faces of the fans made this one of the most worthwhile victory laps you can imagine.

Coach Spurrier did something that day he'd wanted to do since he played at Florida in the 1960s: He led the crowd in a chant of "We're Number 1! ... We're Number 1!" And I got to do something I've always wanted to do: I got to help Mr. TwoBits lead his famous Gator cheer.

It was an emotional day, for sure. A bunch of us got up to speak, and when my turn came, I was overcome by the moment. Usually, when I stand up on a stage to give a speech, I have an idea of what I want to say, and all the right words just sort of come to mind. But this time was different. I was momentarily

I went scuba diving after winning the National Championship and the Heisman Trophy. It was one of the few quiet places I could find.

frozen, overwhelmed by all the adulation and joy of the fans and the camaraderie and closeness of our team.

I remember when they introduced me and everybody was applauding, I looked over to where my teammates were sitting. Except they weren't sitting. One by one, the entire team stood up and clapped. Wow, you want to talk about a moment I'll always remember. As a team, we accomplished so much together and won a lot of trophies and titles, but this was one of the most special times of all. In the midst of all that had happened, it really touched my heart to know my teammates had this sort of respect and admiration for me.

The words that came out of my mouth up on stage that day are as true now as they were then:

"I don't even think I'll try to say how special this is. I'm at a loss for words. I really underestimated the loyalty and the excitement.

"It feels good to feel good."

FROM FUN 'N' GUN
TO TOP GUN

Overly dramatic writers and commentators often used the term "aerial assault" to describe our offense at the University of Florida, but I got a chance to experience some real aerial aggression after our season was over. For public relations purposes, the Air Force sometimes allows well-known civilians to go up for a ride in F-16 fighter jets. Shortly after we won the national title, I not only got a chance to go up in an F-16, I actually flew a final mission with one of dad's friends who was retiring as an air force colonel.

My dad and I were both invited to go along, and it was one of the most amazing experiences of our lives. Taking off was maybe the most awesome aspect of the trip. I've experienced acceleration at high levels with cars, fast motorcycles and watching Ike and Reidel get off the line of scrimmage, but none of that compares with going from zero to a million miles per hour in only a few seconds in a fighter jet.

There were four planes flying in the mission, and at one point they were conducting two-on-two dog-fighting drills. My dad and I felt like Maverick and Goose going after the MIGs in the *Top Gun* movie. On the way back to base, I even got a chance to fly the plane at one point and somehow was able to execute a loop-d-loop and several barrel rolls.

Maybe I missed my calling. If I had another life to live, I'd really consider becoming a fighter pilot.

FLYING HIGH, SINKING LOW

My senior season was both rewarding and chaotic, and I don't think I expected what a whirlwind my life would become.

A few weeks after the national championship, I even got a chance to play golf at Augusta National with one of the members. It was three weeks before they played the Masters there, and the place was gorgeous. The azaleas were beautiful, the magnolias were magnificient and the course was immaculate—until ol' Danny Duffer here got out there and plowed it up. A few times, I wasn't sure if I was taking divots or welcome mats. Afterward, the Green Jackets said I was welcome to play Augusta National again, but they urged me to play after the Masters the next time.

From flying fighter jets to playing world-class golf courses to winning national championships and Heisman Trophies to exploring business opportunities and getting ready for the NFL draft, the pace of my life was hectic and frenzied.

A couple of months after the Sugar Bowl, my family took a week-long vacation to the Keys. That first day, my dad and I went scuba diving, and I dove down about 20 feet beneath the surface. At the time, it seemed like the most quiet, peaceful place in the world. After all the hype and hullabaloo of the last few months, I just sat there motionless under the water. I didn't try to swim, I didn't try to spear any fish; I just sat there in the cool, quiet water.

After about 10 minutes, I started to swim up to the surface, but I changed my mind, did a forward somersault and went back for 10 more minutes of sitting there in complete and utter solitude.

REFLECTIONS

As I look back at the 1996 season, I'm overwhelmed with joy and gratitude. I've heard that in order to accomplish great things, you gave to be in the right place at the right time with the right people. Well, Gainesville was the right place, 1996 was the right time, and did we ever have the right people. From the Head Ball Coach down to the volunteer equipment managers, from All-America players down to scout-team walk-ons and from each and every fan who bled orange and blue, the perfect cast was assembled and, for the first time, Gator fans didn't have to "wait 'til next year." We were finally No. 1.

10

THE TROPHY CASE: AWARDS AND HONORS

Honestly, when I think back on my college career, the stories about the individual awards and honors aren't the first things that come to mind. Don't get me wrong, it was an unbelievable privilege to win the Heisman Trophy and all the other prestigious accolades, but the things that matter most and the moments I recall most vividly about the University of Florida deal with the guys I played with and the friends I made along the way.

Nevertheless, I know I will always be remembered for winning the Heisman Trophy. It's like former Florida State quarterback Charlie Ward once said, "No matter what you do or where you go in life, the Heisman always follows you around." It's been 10 years now since I won the Heisman Trophy, and there's no question it's opened several doors and allowed me to keep one leg in the celebrity world. But in a sense, like everything else, Heisman fame is fleeting. People may identify you because of a trophy you won, but you must distinguish yourself by the man that you are.

GENTLEMAN AND A SCHOLAR

The week after winning the SEC Championship Game, I was travelling all over the country to various awards ceremonies. And by the time all the dinners and banquets were over, I was drained—almost as if I'd been eluding Florida State's pass rush for four quarters. It reached a point where I was doing step-ups on hotel-room chairs and push-ups and sit-ups on hotel-room floors to try to stay in shape for the upcoming Sugar Bowl.

The madness started the Monday after the SEC Championship Game with a trip to New York for the College Football Foundation's functions. After that, it was final exams back in Gainesville and the ESPN College Football Awards Show in Orlando, the Johnny Unitas Golden Arm Award dinner in Louisville, Kentucky, back to New York for the Heisman Trophy presentation and back to Gainesville for more exams and graduation.

That week, I was blessed to win the Draddy Award as the nation's top scholar-athlete, the Maxwell Award (Player of the Year), the Davey O'Brien (Top Quarterback), the Walter Camp Award (Most Outstanding Player), the Honda Scholar-Athlete Award and the Johnny Unitas Award. All the awards were special, but I was especially proud to win the scholar-athlete awards because they recognized contributions and accomplishments on the field and in the classroom.

When I first enrolled at the University of Florida, I have to admit it was an intimidating place for a student-athlete. In high school, we had 25 or 30 students in a class, but at UF as a freshman there were sometimes 300, 400, even 500 students in one huge auditorium for a class. In fact, one class I took had so many students enrolled, it was taught on a big projection screen by a professor who'd taped his lecture earlier in the day.

Thankfully, the University of Florida was very proactive in helping athletes achieve success in the classroom. There was an

Several of my trophies on display for a banquet shortly after my senior season. *(Photo courtesy of Florida Sports Information)*

Office of Student Life, tutors, study halls, and everything you could want or need to become a successful student. I was very fortunate to have attended a university that had the resources and commitment to help me fulfill my academic goals and earn my degree in public relations. At UF, they take great pride in not just making athletes, but turning out scholar-athletes.

I have to admit, though, I did feel stupid when I checked into the Waldorf-Astoria, the landmark hotel in midtown Manhattan, on the night I won the Draddy Award. The hotel was obviously much more grandiose and upscale than I was used to. I left the room to go the banquet, and when I returned I was shocked to see that somebody had been sleeping in my bed and my bags were missing. I didn't think Goldilocks was in New York at the time, so I quickly called security. When they came up, they started laughing. I didn't know that at luxury hotels, they turn down your bed and put your bags in the closet.

Some scholar-athlete, huh?

Another funny thing happened on the day before I won the Heisman Trophy. I was in Louisville, Kyentucky to accept the Johnny Unitas Award. When I was introduced and stepped up to the dais to get the trophy, a woman accidentally tripped and toppled from the stage. Naturally, I raced down to see if she was OK, and thankfully she was. That set the stage for one of my greatest ad-libs ever. When I got back up to the podium, I deadpanned, "They told me if I won all these awards, people would be falling at my feet, but this is ridiculous."

HEISMAN HYPE

I finished third in the Heisman Trophy balloting as a junior, which meant I received an unbelievable amount of preseason Heisman hype heading into my senior year. I can honestly say that the hype never got to me because I never allowed it to.

Earlier in my junior year, I took the television out of my room and I never read a newspaper or magazine article about me for the remainder of my college career. I always felt that much of the pressure you feel internally comes from hearing too many external voices. That's why I decided to cut myself off from watching and reading about our team. The media is usually overly critical or overly positive—and neither one of those options is constructive. The media will pump you up to a point where you get full of yourself or cut you down to a point where you start to question yourself. I decided that the best solution was not to pay attention at all and listen only to the voices that mattered: The voices of God, family, friends, and coaches.

TEAM HEISMAN

The one thing I wanted to make clear when I stood up to accept the Heisman Trophy was this: As great an honor as it was to win the award, it paled in comparison to a living and loving relationship with Jesus Christ. That's why I started my speech with, "I just want to give all the glory and praise to God. He is the rock upon which I stand. Publicly, I'd like to ask Him to forgive me of my sins, for they are many."

And I also wanted to make it clear that it wasn't just Danny Wuerffel winning the Heisman Trophy, it was the Florida Gators winning the Heisman Trophy. Which is why after we won the Sugar Bowl, I had "Team Heisman" hats made and passed them out to all my teammates just to reiterate to them how much they were a part of the Heisman, too.

COACH SPURRIER DOING THE MACARENA?

Probably my most lasting memories from the Heisman weekend involve spending time with the special people in my life. The day after the Heisman ceremony, the folks from the Downtown Athletic Club rented a limo for us and told me and my family we could go anywhere we wanted in New York City. We went and walked around Central Park, played in the famous FAO Schwarz toy store and took a tour of the World Trade Center.

That Sunday night there was a small banquet with all the former Heisman winners and their families. It was a fun night of great food, good music and questionable dancing. For one of the few times, I got to see Coach Spurrier, who'd won the Heisman exactly 30 years earlier, step out of his coaching role

I'm posing with the Davey O'Brien Trophy, the award given to the nation's top quarterback. *(Feragne Portrait Studio of Colleyville)*

and really enjoy himself. I'll never forget watching him slow dance with my mom or doing the Macarena with my sister. After witnessing the Macarena episode, let me just say this about Coach Spurrier as a dancer: He's a tremendous play-caller.

The next night, a Monday night, was the big Heisman fund-raising, black-tie banquet, but the highlight of the night was when we returned to the Downtown Athletic Club. There was a musician performing in the lounge, and when she took a break, I sat down and started playing the piano. Normally, I'm not so bold, but, hey, I'd just won the Heisman Trophy and I was the man of the hour. While I played, my mom came up and

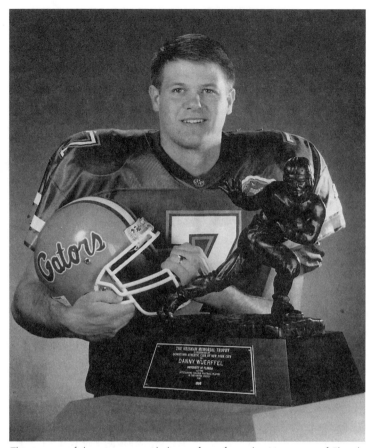

This is one of the promotional shots of me from the University of Florida with the Heisman Trophy. *(Photo courtesy of Florida Sports Information)*

started singing. She started off with "Unchained Melody," the old classic by the Righteous Brothers. My mom has such a beautiful voice and probably could have had a music career, but chose to invest herself in her family and singing in the church. It wasn't long before the entire lounge was rocking with George Rogers (the former Heisman Trophy winner from South Carolina) and my mom singing "Lean On Me" while everybody in the place swayed and sang along.

Speaking of singing, I even had a member of the media sing me a song that weekend. Dave Sheinin, who covered the Gators then for the Miami Herald, serenaded me with a surprisingly stellar rendition of "Danny Boy." Turns out Dave was a music major at Vanderbilt and had an excellent operatic baritone. This was a watershed moment for me because it was the first time in my life I'd ever encountered a sports writer with any real talent.

I'm kidding, of course. I always got along well with the media. I figured if I tried to help them out as much as I could; they would do their best to be fair with me. There were many positive articles written about me after I won the Heisman and, in fact, my co-author for this book, Mike Bianchi, wrote one of them for the *Florida Times-Union*.

Here it is:

NEW YORK—The muggings at Central Park stopped yesterday. The cavalcade of cab drivers at Broadway and 42nd smiled, braked and allowed other cars to get in line ahead of them. The subways were suddenly clean and safe. And the tabloids were responsible.

Danny Wonderful was in town.

University of Florida quarterback Danny Wuerffel, the patron saint of college football, came to New York yesterday to pick up the Heisman Trophy, and while he was at it, he fed the hungry, sheltered the homeless and provided hope for the hopeless (see: Jets).

All right, so I'm exaggerating, but it sure seemed that way last night when the Wuerffel peace train pulled into the Big Apple to collect the most famous award in all of sports. Not that they didn't talk about Wuerffel being the most efficient passer in college football history last night at the Heisman ceremony. Not that they didn't talk about his 114 touchdown passes or his seven miles of career passing yardage. Sure they did. But mostly they talked about the character and the class of a young man whom Florida fans have taken to calling Danny Wonderful.

"There are givers and there are takers in this world, and Danny's a giver," said Florida offensive line coach Jimmy Ray Stephens, who coached Wuerffel at Fort Walton Beach High School. "I don't think Danny could have an enemy. He's the kind of kid you live your whole life hoping your daughter can one day marry. He's sincere, polite, trustworthy, helpful, pretty much all the things they teach you in Boy Scouts."

Wuerffel had already won the Draddy Academic Award, the Walter Camp Award, the Davey O'Brien Award, the Maxwell Award, the Honda National Scholarship Award, the Johnny Unitas Golden Arm Award and, yes, he even won the U.S. Postal Service Player of the Year Award.

Now, he has added the Heisman to his arsenal of awards with the Nobel Peace Prize for Physics next on his agenda.

Last night culminated a hectic week for Wuerffel and his entourage, which included his family, UF officials and Florida coach Steve Spurrier. Before the Heisman ceremony yesterday, Spurrier and his family visited the Statue of Liberty, where Spurrier reportedly welcomed beleaguered immigrants into the country by showing them the tape of FSU's late hits against Wuerffel. No word yet on whether Spurrier took the ferry across New York Harbor or opted to walk.

In all seriousness, this was a night when everybody shared their favorite Danny stories. Like the one from Friday night when Wuerffel was in Louisville to accept the Johnny U. Golden Arm Award. During the presentation, a woman tripped and fell five feet off the back of the stage. Wuerffel jumped up from his seat, picked the lady up and brushed her off. When it was clear she was OK, Wuerffel cracked: "They told me if I won all these awards that people would be falling at my feet, but this is ridiculous."

My favorite Wuerffel story happened a few weeks ago in Nashville when *Times-Union* colleague Matt Hayes and I ran into Danny in the lobby of the team hotel. He was heading back to his room after dinner with a cupful of candy in his hand.

"What have you got there—M&Ms?" I asked.

Wuerffel, without hesitation, extended the cup toward us. "Yes," he replied. "Would you like some?"

That's Danny Wonderful.

Spurrier, admittedly, has tried to make Danny less wonderful, but to no avail. A few weeks ago, Spurrier attempted to convince his star quarterback to occasionally turn down those distracting fans who flock to Wuerffel, robbing him of his time and seeking his autograph on every piece of Gator paraphernalia imaginable.

Wuerffel dutifully nodded at his coach as if to say, "Yeah, you're right." And then he went on being his disarmingly accommodating self.

When Spurrier fumed about the late hits after the FSU game, he told Wuerffel he needed to become angrier and uglier when an opposing defender takes an unnecessary shot. "It's no use," Spurrier said a few days later. "It's against Danny's nature to be mean to anybody."

Spurrier was one of several former Heisman winners present at the dusty ol' Downtown Athletic Club last night to pay tribute to Wuerffel. One notable absentee was O.J. Simpson, who has been nationally vilified since those horrible murders.

The Juice should have come last night.

A little Danny Wonderful might have rubbed off on him.

11

FAITH AND FOOTBALL

A LITTLE PRAYER OF THANKS

During my sophomore season, after sitting on the bench for half the year behind Terry Dean, I finally got a chance to play when we fell behind Auburn late in the third quarter. We were ranked No. 1 in the country and it was a high-pressure situation. My adrenaline was pumping and I was pretty nervous. On my first series, I rolled right to throw a short out route. The cornerback tried to cheat up and make a play, but I saw him at the last second. I pump-faked the out and lofted the ball down the sideline to the clear-out receiver. The free safety came flying over from the middle of the field to try to break up the pass, but he arrived a moment too late; the ball made it just in time for a TD.

Without any planning or forethought, my hands went together for a prayer of thanks—I was overwhelmed with gratitude. And that began what sort of became my trademark. Lots of people still remember me as the QB who put his hands together and prayed after every TD.

It's probably no secret that I'm a Christian. Those who know me—even those who only know a little about me—know that my faith plays an important role in my life. But it's so much more than just a role to play. My faith is not just something I do; it's who I am.

I grew up in a wonderful family. My father was an Air Force Chaplain and I was raised in a Christian home. I never really struggled with the question, "Does God exist?" I knew He existed because we talked to Him before every meal; we thanked Him for His provisions in our lives and we were very aware of His influence on our family. My questions were more along these lines: "What is God like? What's the nature of my relationship with God? What does authentic faith look like?"

When I was growing up, I thought being a good kid was the same as being a good Christian. In my mind, faith was about being a good and moral person, so that's what I tried to be. I avoided the major pitfalls of high school—drinking, drugs, and so forth. But that's not all there is to it. In fact, if you take your faith, boil it down to the basics and are left with simply an exhortation to be a good, moral person hoping to please God and earn his favor, you've really missed the whole point. I learned this lesson during my time at UF.

When I first arrived on campus, I met a guy who worked with a Christian athletic ministry, Athletes in Action (AIA). He met with athletes on campus and taught one-on-one Bible studies, helping young men and women to mature in their faith. I'm embarrassed about this now, but at the time, my attitude was, "I'm really excited about what you are doing, but I'm already on the team. And there are other guys around here that need your help more than I do." What an arrogant and self-righteous attitude! As long as we're breathing, we haven't arrived. We can always mature on our journey of faith. There's plenty of room for growth in all of us.

FELLOWSHIP OF CHRISTIAN ATHLETES

One of the greatest influences in my life has been the Fellowship of Christian Athletes (FCA). As soon as I enrolled in the University of Florida, even though I sort of snubbed the guy from AIA, I started attending FCA meetings, hearing great speakers and meeting many wonderful people. I believe countless athletes and students at UF have been deeply impacted through the Wednesday night meetings, weekly Bible studies and summer camps.

Through the FCA, I met Pete Robertson, who ended up playing a key role in my life. Pete and his wife, Susie, became like second parents to me and were instrumental in my development as a Christian man. There are no words that could express my heartfelt gratitude for the guidance and love that the Robertson family lavished on me during my time in Gainesville. In fact, during my Heisman acceptance speech, the comment "quack, quack, quack" was an inside joke just for Pete and Susie.

Pete and I met weekly for a Bible study that challenged my view of the character of God, and that led to the biggest turning point in my life as a Christian. The scene from the movie *The Lion King* best illustrates how God grabbed hold of my life and began transforming my heart.

THE LION OF JUDAH

Simba, the young lion cub and heir to the throne, was trapped by the wild and dangerous hyenas. In the face of danger, he did what any lion would; he roared. The only problem was it sounded more like a kitten's purr, and the hyenas got quite a laugh. When he went to purr again, something incredible happened. Simba's father, Mufasa, the great Lion King, showed up and his roar was deafening. The demeanor of the hyenas changed in an instant. They were no longer dealing with a small cub; they had the king of the beasts to reckon with.

Most of us are only comfortable with a tame God—a God we can manage. We naturally want to see God as a much smaller entity than He really is—and so we find numerous ways to minimize His greatness. It's much safer to deal with smaller lions. Blaise Pascal, a 17th century mathematician and philosopher, said, "God made man in His image, and man returned the favor." Could it be that we actually conjure up our own image of a God we can deal with and halfheartedly worship our own small deity to get some sense of peace and comfort? As I grew in my understanding of God, I felt like the hyenas when they encountered Mufasa—I had encountered greatness, and my demeanor and attitude drastically changed.

God is so powerful. His incredible might and ceaseless love transcend our understanding. Yes, He is the lamb of God, but He's also the Lion of Judah, infinitely greater than Mufasa.

As my awareness of God's holiness and power grew, I began to see my true self—not so powerful and far from holy. You see, in the presence of someone so large, you realize how small you really are; in the presence of overwhelming strength, you grasp how weak you are. And in the presence of One so pure and holy, all your attempts to be righteous, the best you have to offer, doesn't even begin to measure up.

For the first time, I discovered many of my good qualities were rooted in selfish motives and many of the things people admired about me were superficial, often for public consumption. I was deeply humbled. I had fallen short and suddenly realized I was a chief candidate for God's grace and mercy. The old hymn, "Amazing Grace," became the cry of my heart, recognizing I would be nothing without the tender mercy and love of the Father.

DANIEL IN THE DAWG'S DEN

When I was a junior, we played "Between the Hedges" at the University of Georgia—the first time the Gators had played in Athens since 1932. They were rebuilding the stadium in Jacksonville for the NFL's expansion Jacksonville Jaguars, so my sophomore year we played Georgia in Gainesville and my junior year we played the 'Dawgs in Athens. We went out for warm-ups, and as I mentioned earlier, I'm really not a great pregame player, but on that day I was particularly awful. I started warming up with Brian Schottenheimer, and I was throwing the ball horribly. I tried to remember all the techniques and fundamentals of throwing a football—following through, stepping to your target, transferring weight, and a lot of other mechanical mumbo-jumbo. It didn't help. So I tried throwing the ball harder, thinking that might straighten things out. No such luck. Then I tried throwing it softer; that didn't help either. Finally, Coach Spurrier came up to me and said, "Dang, Danny, what's the matter with you?"

The problems continued when we teamed up with the receivers. I was throwing the ball all over the place—over their heads, at their feet, behind them, in front of them; you name it. Even the receivers started shaking their heads and looking at me funny. Finally, pregame ended and I went back to the locker room really frustrated—about as frustrated as I've ever been on a football field. If a racehorse breaks his leg, he's not really any good to anybody, and they shoot him. It's the same with a quarterback. If he can't throw the ball, he's not really any good for anything else. Fortunately, none of my receivers had a gun in the locker room. At least none that I was aware of.

But in all seriousness, I was frustrated to the point that I got on my knees, and I prayed: "Lord, I've tried everything Coach Spurrier has taught me; I've tried everything I've learned throughout my whole career, and it's not working. If You will help me today, I'll know without a shadow of a doubt that this was a gift from You. I'm turning this game over to You, Lord."

A funny thing happened that afternoon: I had the best statistical game I'd ever played as a Florida Gator (14 of 17 for 242 yards and five touchdowns) and we won the game 52-17. On one of our first drives, I made a bad read and at the last second turned and threw the ball to the opposite side of the field from where I was supposed to throw it. As soon as the ball left my hand, I spotted a Georgia defender standing right in its path for a sure interception. I don't know how it happened—if he miss-timed his jump or what—but the ball went right by him to Ike Hilliard for a touchdown.

Later that game when we were driving deep into Bulldog territory, I scrambled right and tried to throw the ball out of the back of the end zone to avoid a sack, but the defensive end got to me as I was releasing the ball, and it didn't go far enough. Like the other play, I was certain this pass would be intercepted too. I was fully prepared to get up, try to make the tackle and help Coach Spurrier pick up his visor. But, oh no; my man Chris Doering was "streaking" across the back of the end zone and caught the pass for a touchdown. Coach Spurrier asked me how in the world I ever saw Chris. I simply said, "Coach, it's all about peripheral vision." It took years before I finally came clean.

I don't tell that story because I think God is like a genie, granting us wishes and scrambling to satisfy our fleeting desires. I've prayed similar prayers prior to some bad performances as well. But I believe God taught me a valuable lesson in Athens: At some point, after we've tried everything and still fallen short, we've got to get on our knees and say, "Lord, I've tried it all and it's not working. I give my life to You. All that I am or ever will be, whatever might happen, it will all be for Your glory."

NO THANKS, PLAYBOY

There was quite a bit of publicity about a decision I made prior to my senior season when I was nominated to be *Playboy Magazine*'s National Scholar Athlete of the Year. The honor carried with it a trip to a Phoenix resort for a photo shoot with other members of the Preseason All-America Team and a $5,000 gift to Florida's scholarship fund. While I was certainly flattered to be nominated for the award, I declined because I simply felt it was the wrong thing for me to do. I've never claimed to be perfect, and I'm well aware of the blemishes in my character and the defects in my heart. But despite my brokenness, my overriding passion is to bring glory to God in all I do, and going to Phoenix didn't seem to be a good fit. People made a big deal about my decision, but, really, there was no decision to be made.

ONWARD CHRISTIAN SOLDIERS

I often hear people say Christians don't make for good football players because they lose the killer instinct necessary for such a violent sport. I couldn't disagree more. I believe a true Christian should be the toughest player on the field. In the Bible, the greatest warriors were people fully committed to God, and I can think of countless athletes whose intensity, aggressiveness, and dominance increased when they realized they were playing not for themselves, but to glorify God.

However, before I understood this, I mistakenly entered my senior year with a faulty notion of how I was to approach a football game. In our first game (we played Southwestern Louisiana), I was too relaxed and played very poorly, even though we won, 55-21.

Coach Spurrier thought I struggled because the preseason media hype had gotten to my head—the newspaper articles, TV shows, and all the chatter about the Heisman Trophy. I tried to explain to him that I didn't pay attention to the media. Like I already mentioned, during my junior year, I took the television out of my room and quit watching TV altogether. And I never read a newspaper or magazine article for the rest of my career. I told coach I hadn't seen or heard any of the hype, but I'm not sure he bought it.

His solution was to ban me from the media before the next game. Someone showed me the headline of one of the articles about it:"Spurrier Gags Wuerffel." It was really kind of humorous, because I don't believe the media had any bearing on my performance the week before. Anyway, the following week, I came out more intense and aggressive. I didn't join the pregame head butt crew, but I had a very aggressive mind-set. I completed 15 of 16 passes against Georgia Southern and we won, 62-14. To this day, I still think Coach Spurrier blames the media for my poor start.

A CALM IN THE EYE OF THE STORM

In 1996, the day before the Tennessee game in Knoxville, I was reading Oswald Chamber's spiritual devotional, *My Utmost for His Highest*. I came across this passage:"The secret of a Christian's life is that the supernatural becomes natural to him as a result of the grace of God, and the experience of this becomes evident in the practical everyday details of life, not in times with intimate fellowship with God."

And then the following sentence absolutely blew me away and would also prove to be prophetic: "And when we come in contact with things that create confusion and a flurry of activity, we find to our own amazement that we have the power to stay wonderfully poised even in the center of it all."

The next day we played Peyton Manning and the Tennessee Volunteers in what was billed the Game of the Century (again, we played in about three or four of these so-called "games of the century" in one year). It was raining outside and I often had trouble throwing a wet ball. On the opening series of the game, we faced a fourth and 11 from Tennessee's 35-yard line. We called a timeout and decided to go for it. There were 107,000 fans there that day—the largest crowd in NCAA history—and, believe me, they were going berserk! Coach Spurrier's mind was racing and his eyes were jumping back and forth as he tried to figure out what play to call. As I was standing there in the midst of the chaos, Oswald Chambers's line came to me: "We find to our own amazement that we have the power to stay wonderfully poised even in the center of it all."

I don't know if I've ever had a pure vision or a clear epiphany, but what happened next is as close as I've come: While everything and everyone around me was consumed with the magnitude and the chaos of the moment, I looked over and, in my mind, saw Jesus standing by the tunnel that went out of the stadium. He simply looked at me with soft and loving eyes. And while this was happening—the crowd screaming, Coach Spurrier pacing and the rain falling—I saw Jesus turn, go into the tunnel and walk out of the stadium. In my own mind, while Coach Spurrier was calling the play in the midst of the tumult and the shouting, I turned, walked across the field and followed Jesus out of the stadium. Didn't run, didn't trot, just walked after Him and left the madness behind. It was such a freeing and amazing feeling to know that in the midst of one of the most pressurized situations in college football, I was absolutely content to be a part of it—or not be a part it. I didn't have to have it; I didn't need it; it wasn't my obsession. Football was, well, it was just football. Now that is a liberating thought! Then

Coach Spurrier called a post pattern, I threw a long touchdown pass to Reidel Anthony and we went on to win the game, the national championship, the Heisman Trophy, everything.

When we're not paralyzed with the fear of failure or the criticism of others, when we realize we're playing for an audience of One (who happens to be the God of the universe), when we learn to focus on eternal things, things that will last longer than a 30-minute *SportsCenter* episode (even with five straight re-runs), that's when we have the ability to live with a true sense of freedom and security. I have no doubt that my faith not only provided a foundation for life, but actually helped me to be the best football player I could be.

THE DESIRE OF MY HEART

Shortly after I was drafted into the NFL and moved to New Orleans in 1997, I met a wonderful young woman, Jessica Krause. She was living in Florida at the time working for Habitat for Humanity. A mutual friend introduced us, and after several months of late night phone calls and occasional visits, she moved to the Big Easy. A few months later, we got married at a small church on Canal Street. Little did she know that she had boarded a ship that wouldn't dock for quite a while. We moved 13 times in our first four years of marriage chasing down a NFL dream. And after having our first child—Jonah William Wuerffel on December 3, 2003—we prayed together and decided enough was enough.

Without question, our faith has led us through our football career (I say "our" because Jessica experienced every bit as much of the highs and lows as I did. In fact, I think the blind-side blows hurt her more than me and the many sudden moves and cross-country relocations certainly took a higher toll on her). But our faith has also carried us beyond football.

My wife, Jessica, and I enjoy the view by the front range of the Rocky Mountains.

After seven years in the National Football League, we have retired to work at Desire Street Ministries (DSM) in New Orleans. DSM is a non-profit, faith-based organization focusing on spiritual and community development in one of our nation's toughest and poorest neighborhoods. Ever since I was drafted by the New Orleans Saints in 1997, I have been working in this impoverished community in various roles. In only 14 years, DSM has started a pediatric clinic, a church, a school, and much more. The school, Desire Street Academy (DSA), currently provides 150 children with the finest education available and also shapes their character so they will be positive forces in this community for years to come.

I've now gone to work at Desire Street full time, working with the athletic programs and directing the development office. I feel a real sense of purpose and joy working in the ministry with these kids, and I'm excited about what the future holds.

Mo Leverett, the founder and director of DSM, is also a talented musician with six CDs. Like many athletes, I'm a wannabe musician. So Mo encouraged me to get some of my talented musician friends and make a Christmas CD. I thought he was nuts, but that's what led to the making of Heaven and Nature Sings: Christmas with Danny Wuerffel, family, and friends.

What started as a joke ended up, at least in my opinion, a pretty good Christmas CD with some high-quality music. Andrew Copeland and Ken Dew from the popular group Sister Hazel performed a couple of songs, and several other fine musicians added their touches as well. However, we had to include one crazy tune featuring several of my old Gator cronies.

In what was their musical debut and finale all at once, James Bates, Lawrence Wright, and Jason Odom joined me as we sang a Gator rendition of "Go Tell it on the Mountain." James sang a solo dedicated to the Tennessee Volunteers, Lawrence added some soul with a rap, I sang and played the harmonica, and Jason smiled and looked big. Not the finest Christmas tune ever produced, but we sure had a lot of fun doing it. And all the proceeds from the CD benefited the kids at Desire Street Ministries.

For more information about Desire Street Ministries, please visit our website:www.desirestreet.org

BIBLE STUDY

As you might expect, the Bible is my favorite book and one of my most treasured possessions. I believe that God has acted and spoken throughout history, and He has provided us what we truly need to know in the pages of the sacred scriptures. Time and time again, I have found God's word to be true, providing a complete framework to understand the world in which we live. I can't think of any aspect of my life that hasn't been impacted by the message and teachings of the Bible. Here

I always enjoy spending time with the kids at Desire Street Ministries. *(Photo courtesy of Jessica Leigh/The Times)*

are a few of my favorite passages that have meant a lot to me over the years:

Proverbs 3: 5-6. "Trust in the Lord with all your heart, and lean not on your own understanding; in all your ways acknowledge him, and he will make your paths straight."

We tend to give the Lord a little bit here and there, but never really give Him everything and trust Him with all our hearts. To "lean not on your own understanding" implies that you have one—we shouldn't turn our brains off and expect God to work everything out. But the emphasis of the verse is that we are to ultimately lean on God's wisdom, not our own. In all facets of our knowledge and in every aspect of our lives, we need to let Him direct our path. That's what I've tried to do, and it's astounding to look back at the great gifts God has provided me and how He really has directed my path.

1 Samuel 16: 7. "The Lord does not look at the things man looks at. Man looks at the outward appearance, but the Lord looks at the heart."

We are so consumed with the external things in life, especially when it comes to people—what they look like, what their statistics are, what their resume is, how much money they make and so on. We need to be reminded that God isn't impressed with the things we notice. God cares about our character, and He looks at our heart. We would be wise to look more at what really matters.

Hebrew 10: 24-25. "And let us consider how we may spur one another on toward love and good deeds. Let us not give up meeting together, as some are in the habit of doing, but let us encourage one another."

Many people think their journey of faith is a private matter, and that's partially true. There are aspects of our relationship with God that are uniquely private, and there are things that only He will ever know about us. But I've always felt that significant growth rarely happens for spiritual lone rangers—we need to be connected to others. Involvement in a Christian community, in spite of its imperfections, is key to producing genuine spiritual growth. The greatest treasures in my life are the many wonderful people who have loved, accepted, guided, challenged and, if need be, confronted me.

YOU DON'T NEED A CELL PHONE TO CALL GOD

Several years ago, I got the opportunity to demo a Nextel cellular phone to determine whether I wanted to purchase it or not. The phone was amazing; it had all the technological bells and whistles of the time. It had a flip top before they were common, a two-way walkie-talkie and a speakerphone. The

Here I'm recording the Gator rendition of "Go Tell It on the Mountain" with Gator teammates from L to R: James Bates, Jason Odom, Lawrence Wright.

phone used both digital and analogue towers, had no long distance charges and no roaming fees. In about 20 minutes, I thought I'd become a self-made expert on Nextel phones and was really impressed with myself.

Later that week, I met a man who was using what I thought to be an inferior cell phone. In an effort to be a good neighbor, I gently began to instruct him about the new era of cellular service. He tried to say something, but I kept right on going and didn't miss a beat. I told him all about the features— the flip top, the walkie-talkie capability, everything. And then I asked, "Do you know anything about cellular towers and how that stuff works?" As he started to say something, I interrupted him again, telling him about Nextel's nationwide calling plan and the difference between digital and analogue towers. When I finally finished my spiel, I felt certain that if a Nextel executive was around, he would hire me to be a national spokesperson.

James Bates and I had fun goofing around during the recording.

I later asked the man what he did for a living. He said he recently retired as a chief engineer for Nextel, and he had designed and built the phone I'd just finished telling him all about. After retiring, he became an independent contractor, helping companies design and construct cellular towers. You can imagine how embarrassed I felt to have just told the man who created the phone how it worked.

And yet isn't that exactly what we do with God? He created us and knows what's best, but we think we've got all the answers. We think His ways are confining, likening Him to a cosmic killjoy out to rob us of our precious freedom. But the opposite is true. Jesus says in John 10:10, "I have come that they may have life, and have it more abundantly." When we ignore His guidance and feel qualified to steer our own ship, we end up trading abundant life and true joy for a cheap substitute, one that can never satisfy.

C.S. Lewis says in *Mere Christianity*: "If we consider the unblushing promises of reward and the staggering nature of the rewards promised in the Gospels, it would seem that Our Lord finds our desires not too strong, but too weak. We are half-hearted creatures, fooling about with drink and sex and ambition when infinite joy is offered to us, like an ignorant child who wants to go on making mud pies in a slum because he cannot imagine what is meant by the offer of a holiday at the sea. We are far too easily pleased."

THE ICING ON THE CAKE

When I look back at my entire football career, I can't imagine that it could have been any better. Someone introduced me at a banquet the other night and read some of my highlights. As I listened, I almost pinched myself to see if I was awake. I found myself thinking, "Who is this guy talking about?"

I'm still dumbfounded to think that I experienced what most kids can only dream of—like the night in New York when I won the Heisman Trophy at the Downtown Athletic Club. I can remember playing catch as a fourth-grader pretending to be Heisman Trophy winner Mike Rozier from Nebraska or Doug Flutie from Boston College. Who would have guessed that one day I'd be behind the podium accepting such a prestigious award?

From my recruiting days at Fort Walton Beach to the Sugar Bowl in New Orleans, all the way from a last-gasp 28-yard TD pass in the Bluegrass of Kentucky to the celebration at Florida Field with 60,000 of my closest friends, my collegiate football career has provided me with the fondest of memories and the best of friends. I've got a room full of trophies, rings, and pictures that remind me that my childhood hopes and dreams actually did come true.

And yet as amazing as it was—it couldn't have been any better—I can honestly say that it couldn't possibly compare to the deep-seated joy that comes from a loving and living relationship with my Lord and Savior Jesus Christ.

When I reflect on my life—one that seemed to intersect the worlds of faith and football—how blessed I am that my football career was just the icing on the cake, and not the cake itself!

I'm not a retired football player who happened to be a Christian. I'm a Christian who, for a few amazing and wonderful years, happened to play football.

AFTERWORD

As I discussed the release of a softcover edition of this book with the publisher, I was asked to write an "afterword." Honestly, since this was my first go-around as an author, I wasn't exactly sure what that meant. Could this be where I make all the corrections and apologize for any errors in the original editions? Or is this where I would add a story or two about any offended family members who previously weren't included, like my sister, Sara?

After several failed attempts, I talked again with John Fishel at Sports Publishing LLC. He clarified the purpose of an "afterword" and encouraged me to write about any significant happenings in my life since the original book was published. Far from simplifying the project, this only complicated the matter, for I've recently been through an overwhelming sequence of life-transforming events—mostly centered on the devastation of Hurricane Katrina and its aftermath.

My wife and I lost nearly everything we owned as our house flooded, and Desire Street Ministries was left under water as well. The terrible flooding in the Ninth Ward scattered all the inner-city kids with whom we worked. All the events around and following this tragedy couldn't fit in the longest possible "afterword," but as I reflect on this last year, especially in relation to my football career at the University of Florida, several important things come to mind.

First, as we began locating our students and learning of the dire living conditions many of them were in, we felt an obligation to provide for them in any way we could. The main problem was, we didn't have a place since our facility was still under water in New Orleans. As we began looking for an alternate location, we found how difficult it would be to find a place suitable and available for a boarding school.

As I was driving to Gainesville for the Florida-Tennessee game, I heard about a 4-H camp in Florida's panhandle that had a facility large enough to house our school. You then can imagine how excited I was to learn the University of Florida managed the camp. A day later, things were set in motion, and, by October 3, Desire Street Academy had a school for 85 displaced kids from New Orleans. We were able to hold a full year of school, and we even fielded athletic teams in football, basketball, baseball, and track. Many thanks to all the folks at the University of Florida and the 4-H program for making this possible—our school is moving to a more permanent campus in Baton Rouge to begin the 2006-2007 school year. We continue to help clean and restore the Desire neighborhood, and we've been blessed to see our ministry begin to replicate in other cities as well.

A second form of encouragement came when the University Athletic Association offered to give us the proceeds from their second pay-per-view game of the season. I was so blessed to receive a $50,000 check for Desire Street Ministries from Athletic Director Jimmy Foley at a booster meeting before a game.

But without a doubt, the most encouragement I received came not from any one place or person, but from the overwhelming love and support bestowed by Gator fans spread all over the country—a group that has come to be known as *The Gator Nation*. I'll never know how many thousand of Gators donated their time, talents, and treasures to help sustain us through such a difficult time, but the outpouring of support has been overwhelming and nothing short of a miracle. At every home game at the Swamp, more than 85,000 fans sing a song that includes a line that best captures my feelings as I reflect on the Hurricane and how the Gator nation stepped up to help one of their own in a time of need:

"... In all kinds of weather, we all stick together ... "

Thanks again to *The Gator Nation*, God Bless, and GO GATORS!

For more information on the continuing story of Desire Street Ministries, please visit www.desirestreet.org.

 One of the greatest players in Florida football history, quarterback Danny Wuerffel won the 1996 Heisman Trophy while leading the Gators to the national championship. During his four-year career, Wuerffel also led Florida to four SEC titles and two national championship games. He is the only Heisman recipient to also receive the Draddy Scholarship Trophy, which is presented by the National Football Foundation and the College Football Hall of Fame to the nation's top football scholar-athlete.

 Coauthor Mike Bianchi is an award-winning columnist for the *Orlando Sentinel*. Bianchi is a University of Florida graduate who worked for the *Gainesville Sun* and the Florida *Times-Union* in Jacksonville before moving to the *Orlando Sentinel*. He cohosts a daily sports talk radio show in Orlando each morning and also takes part in a statewide TV sports talk show on the Sunshine Network.

Celebrate the Heroes of Florida Sports
in These Other NEW and Recent Releases from Sports Publishing!

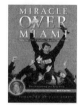